LORD
of the
Hunt

and other tales of grace

LORD
of the
Hunt

and other tales of grace

STEVEN E. ROBINSON

COLLEGE PRESS PUBLISHING COMPANY
Joplin, Missouri

Copyright © 1991
College Press Publishing Company

Printed and Bound in the
United States of America
All Rights Reserved

Library of Congress Catalog Card Number: 90-86281
International Standard Book Number: 0-89900-394-X

to

the Tempe Church of Christ
where I learned to love and be loved.

Author's Note

The events in my life of which I write are true. I cannot presume that any other human being is as shameless as I; therefore, though I wrote the truth about myself, I have taken liberties to conflate times, places and details to conceal others' identities and to honor their privacy. The only person's strivings, failures, joys and sorrows I wish you to know and feel are my own.

TABLE OF CONTENTS

Acknowledgment 11
Introduction 13

PART ONE 1950's
The Knowledge of Good and Evil

1. Sis's Place 19
2. The Gospel Fairy Tale 27
3. The Mitt 33
4. The Greatest Commandment 41

PART TWO 1960's
Making Straight the Way of the Lord

5. The Choosing 51
6. The Betrayal of Jackie 55
7. The Crucifixion of Leslie 63
8. The Election 69
9. The Will of God 77
10. The Man in the Mall 83
11. The Derelict 87

PART THREE 1970's
God Is Love . . .

12. I Was Blind But Now I See   93
13. Second Hand People, Thrift Store Churches   99
14. The Lord of the Hunt   105
15. Remember Me   109
16. How I Am   119
17. Go Home, Child   129
18. The Temptation of Frank   137
19. His Faithfulness is Everlasting   143

PART FOUR 1980's
. . . and Jesus Was a Carpenter.

20. Chaplains All, They Are   151
21. Ralph   159
22. The Gospel According to Steamed Zucchini   163
23. Why, Jake?   167
24. Earthmama and Billy   171
25. Rolling Eyes   175
26. One Night on the Phone   179
27. Broken Legs   187
28. Children . . .   193

CKNOWLEDGMENTS

These are some of the people whom I love and who, at times have loved me more than they know. If not for you I . . . well, I cannot imagine.

Joe Bob and Elaine, friends (the word seems inadequate) who redeemed my life and who first told me I can and should write.

Ben, my Sunday morning breakfast friend and balancing influence.

Tim, my beloved brother who listened for almost a year.

Dr. Jim Beyer, who was honest with me and it made all the difference in the world.

The members of the Eastside church of Christ who never gave up on their "hippie" teenager.

The "Thursday night Bible study group" who never tired of Romans.

The Sunday morning Bible class at the Tempe church of Christ in which I can be honest.

And the last is truly first: my wife, Jan. I'm glad we are growing old together.

NTRODUCTION

Most good books I've read have an introduction. But then, so have most bad ones, too. The books that didn't have an introduction make me feel, well, uncomfortable. Somehow it just doesn't seem proper to go directly from the page that says all the "Library of Congress Number . . . No part of this book may be reproduced under penalty of death blah blah blah" right into the first chapter. It is like walking into someone's house without knocking first. So please spend a moment with me and let me introduce myself and my book to you.

This is a book about the lifelong process of learning grace. It is a collection of stories, true ones, that are really one story: how God relentlessly pursues us, revealing himself to us at every turn of our lives, even the ones that are so dark we cannot (more, do not want to or even dare not) see.

It is within these pages that I tell you some things that only God knew about me two years ago. Writing this book was about as difficult a thing as I have done in my life. Not the mechanics, but the telling of the stories. First, I wrestled often with what seemed to me to be an egomaniacal presumption that what I had to tell about God, about me, and what goes on between us, is worth your time hearing. The second thing, the harder thing, was having the sheer guts to tell the truth about how I came to know my need for grace and how God meets that need. The need for grace is not often a beautiful thing to see, nor can an apt word or a clever turn of a phrase make it so. I say all this guardedly because write, I did. And tell the truth, as much as was within me to tell, I did. I have come to know that the truth of the gospel requires honesty on my part for it to make any sense at all. The truth is "Jesus Christ came to die to save sinners." The honesty required to truly know that truth is "among whom I am foremost of all" (I Timothy 1:15,16).

I think it is best to tell you my reasoning for the divisions of this book, now, before you continue. Within each decade certain events remain forever fixed, like the stars, by which I navigate my journey with God. In broad strokes the fifties are my elementary school years; the sixties, junior high, high school and adoles-

INTRODUCTION

cence; the seventies, one wife, two and a half college degrees, social work, foster parenting, two children and the ministry; and the eighties, my construction company and still the same one wife I had in the seventies. I decided to place events in the time frame they occurred or people in the decade in which I met them, even though their significance may have only occurred to me in the here and now.

As I have told these stories I have found that I tell a lot of people's stories. Not the same incidents but the same joys, sorrows, shame, fear, hopes and needs. The truth I tell you is this: As brutal as our truths get, his grace is sufficient.

To the praise of his glory. . . .

1950'S
PART ONE

THE KNOWLEDGE OF GOOD AND EVIL

CHAPTER ONE
IS'S PLACE

For by grace you have been saved through faith; and that not of yourselves, it is the gift of God....
        Ephesians 2:8

The war within me began on that day. Or it was that on that day I became conscious of the war.

Though I was but five years old (and a half), I am not lost for the remembrance of the event, nor for the feelings I had at the time. Perhaps it was precisely because I was all of five and had no words to put to the experience but could only live within it, wordlessly, for over three decades, that it is present so powerfully in me at this very moment.

THE LORD OF THE HUNT

It was in December of 1957 that I first met my Aunt Sis. Sis was my father's sister. Everyone called her Sis, even my Gran and Ganpa.

We drove the five hours from our house to Gran's where, as usual, I recovered from carsickness while the adults sat and talked in the kitchen around the big picnic table. It was always covered with an oil cloth that made your forearms go "Shhhhhh . . . k!" as you peeled them up from its sticky surface, a basket of leftover biscuits from breakfast, and a perpetually half completed 5,000 piece jigsaw puzzle on one end. It was Christmastime and we were visiting just long enough to pick up our presents to take back home to Memphis across the river. I also got two dollars and a handful of loose change from Ganpa. It came with his standard warning.

Everything I got from Ganpa, whether it was an ice cream before bedtime while Gran took her bath, or a half cup of black coffee with him in the morning while she tended the garden, or quarters from his change at the grocery store, always came with a stern warning, "Now don't you go tell Gran." I never understood the nature of the conspiracy involved but we always grinned knowingly at each other as if the meaning was shared perfectly between us men.

This visit, Dad said, we would stop by Sis's place on the way home. We'd been to Uncle Bill's place and Uncle Joe Bob's place. Sis's place was a new place to me. I looked forward to meeting my Aunt Sis with as much enthusiasm as a carsick five-year-old could muster.

So we drove. And drove. Past farms winter dead, past houses all wooden-gray and bent with years, past overalled old men sitting on front porches with roofs about to collapse in the centers. We passed skeletons of old trucks and tractors, graveyards of cars that seemed to come to certain places to die with their own kind. I began to get carsick again and slumped into the back seat. Then the car slowed. I groped to pull myself up to the window to see where we were.

My belly sloshed dangerously as we turned, bump, roll, toss and jerk onto a dirt road. It was plowed up by the tires that had cut through the dense red clay at the last rain.

At the end of the road was a house. No, not a house, a . . . a . . . I wasn't sure what. It was a wood structure, much like a house, only I wasn't sure if it was a true house. It was a crazy quilt of gray boards, corrugated tin, pieces of sheet metal, and odd size lumber. Old dead washing machines bleeding rust, killed cars, bald tires, drab green 55-gallon drums, tilted farm machinery, and garbage, oh the garbage, littered the landscape. A honk of the horn and the house spewed forth its dirty contents: a woman, heavy, waddling, waving, the flesh hung from her arms swinging like a trapeze, and screeching children of every size, eight I think there were.

THE LORD OF THE HUNT

So, this was Sis's place.

I got out of the car and soon fascination overtook my incredulity. We kids climbed and explored, cranked the rusted cranks, climbed on heaps of machinery, and threw rocks! Yes, we could throw rocks with abandon! There were no windows to break and no neighbors' houses to hit.

We went inside and it was much like the outside only with an air, a thick dank air, but an air nonetheless, of dignity to it. As I looked I began to sense something was terribly, terribly wrong. And it came to me. It was, as a five-year-old's terrors go, a most terrible terror. There was no Christmas tree. There were no presents. There were no red flannel stockings, no cards pinned hanging cattywompus from the corners, nothing red or green or white hung on the walls. There was no Christmas in this place called Sis's.

I will suppose my battle lines were drawn when I heard my father and Aunt Sis talking in low adult tones. "Come on, Sis, take it. At least get something for the kids will you? Of course we can afford it."

It was then that I entered the warfare. I heard something command me with a holy command and at that moment I knew better than I knew my own name what I had to do. It fell upon me, the understanding did, and would not let me go, and has not let me go since. I reached into my pocket and pulled out the two dollar bills my Ganpa gave me. And I tell you now it was without an ounce of pretentiousness, no, with not a hint of desire for reward, but purely from a heart commanded by compassion, I walked up to my Aunt Sis and extended my hand to her with my two dollars in it and said, "Aunt Sis, please buy some Christmas presents with this." She did not take my two dollars. Instead she took me, and I was instantly lost, smothering, crushed to her enormous breasts, my head turned sideways for air, my arms poking crazily from between her rolls of flesh and ham-hock arms. And the woman wept the happiest weeping I ever heard. It was physically as uncomfortable a place as I had ever been, but spiritually, I knew that was where I belonged. I knew graciousness, gratitude, grace. She could have broken all my bones and smothered me blue in the face in her bosom and I wouldn't have cared. I was drunk with the Spirit, filled to overflowing with the divinest of gifts unsought and unasked for.

It was no sooner than my feet touched the ground and I was still swimming in the good ("good" as in "God is good," not "Cookies are good") feeling that enveloped me, that I heard within me another voice, not a true audible voice, but something, like the other, that was compelling, demanding. And I listened to it, and I acted upon it too. And this is true. I had still in my pocket some change. And in plain sight of Aunt Sis and the kids, I fished a nickel from the stack of change in the palm of my hand and held it up. "Here's a nickel," I announced. "Who would like a nickel for Christmas? It's free." The words had no sooner left my mouth that I knew this new voice, this other compelling voice had deceived me, it had damned me. My eyes were opened. I knew good from evil. I fled the house and I hid in the car, huddled in the back seat burning with shame.

I knew, and the knowledge was red hot in every pore of my skinny frame, I had sought to force the hand of grace, to buy the gift of God with my tarnished silver. But I knew, too, it would not have mattered if I had held forth a hundred dollars. I had tried to bring upon myself again by means of a contrived, cheap, egotistical, and selfish deed that very presence of God I loved and desired.

I was wretched. Within moments I had come to know both the wild, holy joy of grace and the burning sword of the angel that would never allow me to return to dwell in innocence again.

And thus my war began.

It is the warfare of the Spirit and the flesh in us all. The Spirit leads, speaks within us a truth to which we cannot close our hearts, and if we will heed the calling we find ourselves compelled to walk in mysterious ways that open up to the very presence of God.

But the flesh also calls to us and speaks in careful lies, half-truths that are sensible, economical, so compelling in their reasonings and believable in their promised outcomes. The flesh knows no mystery, it trusts no paradoxes, it seeks to get and live through its own powers, not to give and die and trust in the resurrection.

At Sis's place, where I became conscious of light and darkness, Spirit and flesh, where I came to know good and evil and the power of graciousness and shame, I learned also the very rudiment of grace: The presence of God, his graciousness cannot be bought at any price. No matter how closely an act may resemble one of goodness or how costly the effort, if it is our own device, grace cannot be had.

Grace is given only in a mystery, at the moments we simply walk by the Spirit, naked in his presence, without pretense, without asking him for or presuming to name a price for his freely bestowed gift.

CHAPTER TWO
THE GOSPEL FAIRY TALE

> *I praise Thee, O Father, Lord of heaven and earth, that Thou didst hide these things from the wise and intelligent and didst reveal them to babes.*
>
> Matthew 11:25

When I was a child. . . .

Let me begin again.

When I was younger, I had a set of children's books I loved, and still do. One of my favorite volumes is "Folk and Fairy Tales." I put away my childish things when I began growing up . . . ; let me restate that. I put away the things of my childhood as I got older and pursued childish things. Owning lots of things. Owning few things (it was a stage I went through.) Impressing people. Seeking spirituality in grown up places and grown up words. Knowing lots and lots of stuff.

So, now I've owned some things, impressed a few people, and know some stuff. In the process I learned the gospel. At first I thought it was a fairy tale. Then I thought it was a way to escape reality. Now I think it is reality. It is the same reality I learned from the brothers Grimm and Hans Christian Andersen in my first childhood.

You see, in the process of becoming grown-ups we all join the ranks of the king and his court who, because they were too proud to admit they were fools would not speak the truth that the emperor in his new clothes was parading stark buck-naked and all were even greater fools in the end for it. But in growing up I still knew deep within, like the king and everyone else, what the truth really is. The truth, spoken by a Child, admonished me to become a child again. In him I understood that reality is as true and as profound as the fairy tales I lived in all those years of rainy days and bedtime stories.

I knew the truth that we all got to go to the grand ball by grace and there, found our true love. I knew too we disobeyed the command and we ran in terror and shame as our garments of silk and splendid coaches and prancing white horses turned to rags, pumpkins and rats. But our Prince sought us and found us, in our rags, amid the rats, living in squalor and took us home with him and married us anyway.

I knew that truth that the Steadfast Tin Soldier endured great misfortunes for the love of the paper dancer. He was cast into the fire because he was rejected and deemed unworthy to be counted among the whole and pretty toys. In the end his love drew the dancer to him in his fiery death, and perishing together they were resurrected as a tin heart that declared to all his everlasting love that fires could not overcome, that many waters could not quench, a love that was stronger than death.

I knew the truth that the Magic Fish granted all things the fisherman's wife desired to make her happy, but when she desired to be like God she lost it all.

I knew the truth that we lost our precious Rapunzel because we desired and ate what was forbidden. I knew too that evil seemed to triumph over the prince who came to rescue the one he loved, the one that was held hostage by evil. But no matter how the evil witch tried to keep them apart, their love drew them together and through tears of sorrow over the wounds endured for the sake of love, a miracle occurred and the two were united forever.

I knew the truth that no matter how ugly a duck we believe we are, how misfit, how rejected and outcast we think we may be, we are created swans, in the image of The Swan, one so graceful and wondrously beautiful. And that image will one day be manifested both to ourselves and the world, not because we were able to make ourselves into acceptable ducks but simply because of The Swan whose graceful image we bear.

And my favorite truth: the truth that love, true love, unconditional love, graceful love will transform the ugliest of beasts into a prince.

These truths struggle for their place against our grown-up notions of reality: that you get what you pay for, you earn your own way, do your best, work hard and you'll succeed, if you're competent, impress the right people, meet the qualifications and stay on top you'll be rewarded, and there's no such thing as a free lunch. These grown-up truths claim the right to replace my childish ideals: that there is mystery at work in the world, a profound order we can speak of only through images, that speaking truth is best, evil gets it in the end, love conquers all, death is only sleep when One who is willing to die for love comes along and kisses us, and that Someone loves me in my ugly beastness and through that love I will some day become fully, perfectly human. Given the choice, I'll take my fairy tales over my dull, bookkeeping adult world, thank you.

The gospel is the most marvelous of all fairy tales. But it is not a tale of imaginary elves and dragons. The gospel is truth, the fulfillment of all human hopes and desires to be saved from the world and even from ourselves by some benevolent Fairy Godmother, some Prince, some Princess, Someone whose love is pure, whose invincible goodness is stronger than the evil of the wicked witch. We know, within the child inside us all, without that fairy tale hope we don't have a hope in the world.

The gospel is the mystery of God told in a foolish tale as real as death, lies, envy, pride, resurrection, hope, love, grace and truth; a mystery only a child would believe. Or an adult who is not ashamed to admit the truth about the emperor's new clothes and himself.

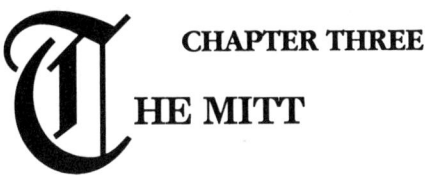

CHAPTER THREE
THE MITT

You did not choose Me, but I chose you....

John 15:16

It was twenty-eight years ago. These are the things I remember about fourth grade. There was the red dirt playground of Saint Williams, my first baseball mitt, Little League and my father's transfer to Taiwan, all that year. Each has finally wrought its conviction; each is just now finishing its work of grace.

Though it has been nearly thirty years I still remember some of my friend's names. Thomas, who had seven brothers and sisters; Vincent, a light brown boy whose origin was an enigma to us all; Sammy, who was held back in first grade; Jack, who sneezed into his hand one day and no one had a Kleenex. And Raymond. Raymond was "retarded" as we were allowed to say back in the fifties.

Recess and P.E. were death for me in elementary school. I was the smallest kid in my classes. If not the smallest I was certainly the least feared. I had to participate in grade school sports during the Dark Ages before the discovery of the fragile self-image, before the light of child psychology was shed on playground dynamics. In those days the biggest, most popular and most powerful kids were usually appointed as team captains and the rest of us were alternately chosen by these gods of the playground to make up their teams. I was not endowed with athletic ability like most of my classmates. I remember standing in the red dust with the group between the team captains, listening to the cheers as one side or the other got a coveted talented, aggressive player, watching the teams fill and the center group dwindle down to the small, the fat, the goony, the bucktoothed and bespectacled misfits until only Raymond and I were left.

I usually stared at the ground too embarrassed to look up because they might see my fear of being the very last in the center; or sometimes I tried to act like I was not particularly concerned about the matter by grinning stupidly while the team captains argued over who HAD to take one or both of us this time. If either of us was ever actually chosen, I, at least, realized it

THE MITT

was purely out of some nine-year-old's version of pity (though I didn't know that word then). Raymond, I still hope and pray, was oblivious to it all and just went where he was told to go.

It was that same year that my father bought me my first baseball glove and signed me up for Little League. We went to the Ben Franklin Five and Dime to shop for a mitt. I knew little about baseball, I was not good at it, I probably hated it (I know I do not care for it now), but I knew that to have an autographed mitt meant a great increase in my likelihood of getting picked sooner by the gods of the game at P.E. If for no other reason, one of the cool guys who was already chosen would always want to borrow it from me and would use his influence to get me picked. Thus I never really used my mitt at recess, since it would end up on someone else's hand in the infield, and I would be assigned to the far outfield where few fourth graders could hit the ball. It was not a critical nor prestigious position to play but it beat getting picked last.

I am right-handed. It made sense to me therefore that I should have a right-handed glove, meaning one that fit on my right hand. My father tried to explain to me that a right-hander catches with his left hand so he can throw with his right, but I would have none of it. I knew the purpose of having a mitt is to catch a baseball. I knew that if I could not catch a baseball with it I would be laughed at. And I just knew I could not catch with my left hand. I would rather have been eternally, mittlessly, but safely, consigned to the outfield than to be humiliated by my ineptness with my new mitt. I never revealed my reasonings to my father, but I was so adamant he bought me the right-handed mitt I wanted. I soon found out he was right and after school, in the seclusion of our back yard, my father chased wild throws all over the yard as I struggled to learn to throw left-handed.

I signed up for Little League at that time and I went to tryouts with my right-handed mitt and a sense of impending doom. One of the coaches noticed immediately that I alternated between my right and left hands and asked me if I could pitch with both hands. To avoid the embarrassment of explaining my stupidity in picking out my glove I said yes, knowing full well I could not even throw well enough with my right hand to hit the dugout, much less get the ball over the plate with my left. I remember his face lighting up. What a find! A switch pitcher! I remember the fleeting elation of having someone impressed by me, of being considered for THE prize position on the team, and the terrible sinking feeling of knowing I would ultimately be found out and surely humiliated. That week my father got orders and we were transferred to Taiwan. Though it meant leaving my friends it also meant I got to quit Little League, mercifully before my dark secret was discovered and I was completely humiliated before the team and my friends at school when the word got around.

So, here I am twenty-eight years later, reading the parables of Jesus Christ and realizing that, just as my

THE MITT

pain about the playground and my mitt speaks to all of us and our own most secret pain, so the gospel holds our hope for us all.

I read in the parables how God goes out into the streets and alleys and calls out the last, the least, the lost, the helpless, the hopeless, and the worthless to play on his team, which wins because of him and is not hindered by the lack of talent in those he chooses (Luke 14:15-24). I read how God chooses the last ones left and makes them the first string of the All Star team (Luke 14:7-11). I read how he takes the rejects, the skinny ones with thick glasses, the oblivious and the ones standing idly on the sidelines, their shirt-tails out, with lunch on their fronts, and inducts them into the Hall of Fame for just standing in the outfield for the last inning (Matthew 20:1-16, all author's paraphrases).

I read the gospels and I saw Jesus with the sinners. As much as it hurt to finally admit it, I understood that I really was, I really am, the last, the worthless, the least, the unchosen, the unwanted. I realized that to deny that painful reality is to deny his grace. I finally understood that my only hope is in the truth of the gospel, that the only ones chosen are those who know they are not worthy of being chosen. I stood off in the distance, I fell on my face before him saying, "God, please choose me; be merciful to me, the sinner."

Twenty-eight years later I understand the gospel and realize too that the Little League and my mitt speak of the killing flaw in my humanity, truly all humanity: It is to seek acceptance through lies and illusions of competence and trumped up abilities. This is woven into the very fabric of our beings. How often I have put on pretenses, overstated my qualifications, my experience, my credentials, inflated a resume, covered up a failure, or tried to make an impression on someone only to lie awake with a knot of dread in the pit of my stomach at being found out.

And we must think about what illusions we might be holding up before God. Do we stand before him and declare, "I am not like the sinners, God. I pray, I fast, I tithe"? Do we come to the Father and say, "I am not like your prodigal sons. I work hard in your house, I do not waste your blessings on worldly pleasures"? What value, what worth, what talent, what competence, what knowledge do we hold up before him as if to make ourselves acceptable to him? We often come to God as if we are trying to qualify somehow for his love and choice of us, like it is a position on his team. (The proper doctrinal mitt or moral bat will get you chosen – this is what it comes down to for most religion.) But at the moments we are able to be honest with ourselves, we tremble at being found out for what we really are: a goony, lonely kid fearful of rejection, with no talent and a wrong-handed mitt.

But we have been found out. God knows. And Jesus calls out our names anyway. You see, he too stood one day, with just two of them left, and the crowd chose the other, Barabbas, not him. There was no one to stick up for him. He was tossed back and forth between Pilate and Herod, the team captains, who argued over who had to take him. He was finally left dead least, hanging between heaven and earth, rejected by both, and he died in the outfield with two other slobbering, rejected misfits.

Now he's the team captain.

He looks into the downcast, awkwardly grinning faces of the skinny, hopeless, worthless misfits who have no autographed mitts, who are hoping against hope to be picked and not be left standing rejected, finally and completely alone, and he knows how they feel. I tell you the truth: as long as he is the one choosing up sides he will never let Raymond, or me, or you, ever be picked last again.

CHAPTER FOUR

THE GREATEST COMMANDMENT

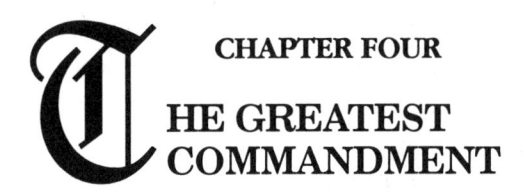

> *And one of them, a lawyer, asked Him a question, testing Him, "Teacher, which is the greatest commandment in the Law?" And He said to him, " 'You shall love the Lord your God with all your heart, and with all your soul, and with all your mind.' This is the great and foremost commandment. And the second is like it, 'You shall love your neighbor as yourself.' On these two commands depend the whole Law and the Prophets.*
>
> *Matthew 22:35-40*

I remember laying out Father Wiley's garments for the Mass. I handled them as though they were the garments of Christ himself. I remember the first Mass I served, my soprano second grade voice mumbling and stumbling through the Latin. I still feel the shiver of awe I had at being at the altar, so close to the sacraments.

I remember I decided to become a priest in that same year. I never fulfilled that desire within the sacraments of the Roman Catholic church. Along my way I exchanged the majestic ritual and awe of the Catholic tradition for the simplicity and literalness of a "Protestant" tradition. I am not here to condemn nor defend either but to bear witness to you of the love of God. I discovered that love during my sojourn in both.

The common thread in my change of beliefs and traditions was my desire to obey the commandments of God. But along my way, somewhere, somehow the commandments themselves became gods, exactness became the criteria for salvation. There was no mystery, all was knowledge, reverence became fear, and humility became spiritual arrogance. In all of this there was a gnawing hollowness. While I was convinced in my mind I was accomplishing something spiritual or being something that God commanded and thus was good, deep within I knew something, somehow, was not good. Something of precious substance, something of great importance was missing in my quest for peace in correctness and perfect obedience.

But somewhere, somehow I discovered mystery and awe again. I found in my life things of inexplicable power and grace. I became a child again; I ceased trying to figure our how the rabbit got in the hat and reveled in the joy of the magic. I ceased trying to understand how we can conjure love from hearts so battered by life and hurt, and just loved people. It was then I understood God. It was then I was at peace. Out of my struggles I offer this to you.

THE GREATEST COMMANDMENT

Jesus says there are really only two commandments. All other commandments are corollary or commentary. The two greatest commandments: fall in love . . . joyfully, passionately, head-over-heels, wonderfully in love with the Lord your God, and have compassion and mercy, forgiveness and grace for your neighbor.

I hear the simplicity of the commandment and my heart fails within me. How can it be?

How can I be commanded to love? How can I bring forth on command the joyful, consuming passion of love? I know I can act as though I love someone. There have been times moral expediency or guilt or fear or lust have commanded me to act like I was in love. Sometimes the act fooled those for whom I acted, sometimes not. In the acting, though, there was no consuming passion, no tears of joyous wonder, no sacrifice of my life beyond the expectation of something of equal or greater value in return, nothing to surprise myself at the depth of the love and desire I had for my beloved.

And how can I be commanded to look at one suffering and feel my stomach wrench in compassion for him? I know I can be coerced by guilt or the desire for praise and acceptance into giving or acting like I am moved by suffering. In all the acting though, my heart can remain selfish, cold and unmoved.

Here, in the simplicity of the commandment, is the root of my distress. I know I cannot be commanded to do the very thing I am commanded to do. The love I know I ought to have for God and my neighbor I cannot bring forth upon demand. Even if the demand is from God himself.

I intuitively understand in other aspects of life I cannot be commanded even to appreciate something, much less love someone. I cannot be told to appreciate Picasso, Debussey, T.S. Eliot, heavy metal rock and roll, French food, or jazz. I cannot be told to worship the ground that someone walks on. I cannot be commanded to adore someone. I know these things about myself (and I assume others are the same way) and yet I have, and so have others, for years blindly accepted the notion that God thinks he can command me to appreciate him and to love him unconditionally and passionately, worship the ground he walks on (or doesn't walk on) and care deeply about his creations.

The problem with accepting the notion that God has actually "commanded" or even issued a strong suggestion that we had better love him and our neighbor (whether that suggestion is for our own good or not is irrelevant here) is that other notions come with the package, much like fleas on a dog. The flea on this dog is that I am supposed to be capable of loving upon command. I know full well I cannot. Even if it is for my own good. And so I struggle with the command and I struggle with my inability to obey fully and love as deeply as it seems God commands I ought.

But here are some other things I have come to understand. These things have opened the mystery of the command. Hear me. There are things of wonder and beauty that move me deeply and incomprehensibly to feelings that I cannot control. I am commanded, in a sense, and I am powerless to disobey. I understand this: to see my best friend for the first time in years is a command to me to smile and be glad. To say goodbye to one I love, to embrace for the very last time in this life is a command to look deeply, wordlessly at one another and feel my deepening emptiness fill with tears. To hear "You are forgiven" after grievously hurting someone I love is a command to be humbled, grateful and at peace within. To see Mother Teresa holding a leprous old man, to see a child hollow eyed and reduced to skin over bones by hunger is a command to feel compassion. When I hear a certain piece of music it is a command to remember that friend, that love, that time when . . . , and to feel just as I did those years ago. The smell of roses, a greasy spoon on a certain street corner, a photograph, a name alone is sometimes a command to rejoice, to be misty-eyed, to smile, to feel a melancholy contentment or to laugh. These command me, not with words, but with wonder and majesty and with beauty that reaches into the depths of my most secret needs and desires and my most sacred memories and deepest hungers.

Perhaps then, it is not that God commands me or tells me I must fall in love with him (like "You WILL eat those peas, young man"), but it is that he simply places himself before me in all of his loveliness, beauty, awesome majesty and gracious mercy. It is that he intends to command me by his very presence, to draw from my heart and soul all the love and devotion and adoration I harbor within me. He does not seek to coerce love from me by directive, but he goes to any length to compel me to adoration and to elicit my love from me. For God to reveal himself to me is in itself the command to love him with all my heart, soul, mind and strength. To be forgiven by Him is the command to have peace. To know his mercy is the command to walk humbly with him in gratitude. To see his heart's desire for my heart is the command to rejoice. To find his love unending and infinite is the command to worship and adore.

Thus, the greatest commandment is not so much a dictate but more the deepest desire of God's heart being expressed to me. "Fall in love with me," is the command of his presence, the compelling message of the cross.

The second greatest commandment is like the first: love your neighbor as yourself. It is like the first because it is also impossible to fulfill by sheer will. It is like the first because it is an overflowing of the first, a command that is rooted in the passion we have for our beloved. This I have come to understand, too.

Being in love commands me to see the world through new eyes. Where there was once nothing of interest there is now delirious beauty. I now see irises and strawberries in a way I never have seen them before. Love commands me to hear music and the wind like I've never heard it before. I feel the temperature of the morning air in a way I have never felt it before. My love commands me to be touched by words and thunder, artichokes and park benches, hot dogs and blue, in ways I have never known because they are shared with my beloved.

So you see, having fallen in love with God, I see the world as through new eyes. Being in love with God is the command to see my neighbor differently. To see someone in need, or hurting or sorrowful or doubting or in pain, this is a command to my heart to be compassionate, forgiving, kind, gracious, and merciful. It is simply what happens because of my heart's deepest love and longing for its Beloved, God. I cannot help it, it just happens inexplicably and powerfully. The presence of the world before me is itself the command to love it and serve it because of the love I have for its creator.

Jesus said, "If I be lifted up, I will draw all men unto myself." From his cross he draws from within me all I am, all I have. All is new, I am my beloved's and he is mine. In his consuming passion he has done what all the finest and best lovers in stories and history have always done. He gave his life to possess me, to win my love.

Yes, the cross is like the old song, the smell of a summer's new mown grass, the distant rumbling of a freight train in the humid night, the sound of an old familiar voice, a friend walking through the door unexpectedly, that draws from somewhere deep within me a remembrance of what once was, and rekindles the fierce desire to know him, a passion for his presence, my love, peace, sometimes a tear of grief, and yes, even a weeping for joy.

1960'S
PART TWO

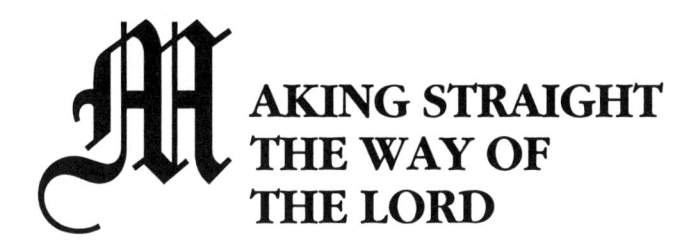

MAKING STRAIGHT THE WAY OF THE LORD

CHAPTER FIVE
THE CHOOSING

> *But the Governor answered and said to them, "Which of the two do you want me to release for you?" And they said, "Barabbas."*
> Matthew 27:21

I don't know about you, but give me the choice and I will usually choose:

the largest cookie in the batch,

two slices of bread from the middle of the loaf instead of the first and slightly stale ones,

to give advice rather than have to ask for it,

the car with gas in it,

to teach rather than to be taught,

the glass of Coke from the new bottle rather than the one poured from the one sitting open all evening,

the slice of pizza with the most pepperoni on it,

the larger piece of cheesecake if only two are left; if there is more I'll slice a little off another,

to be thanked for giving rather than be given to,

the healthiest looking cherry tomatoes for my salad,

the second slice of baloney rather than the slightly slimy one on the top,

the white meat,

an evening with somebody I enjoy rather than with someone who needs an evening to enjoy with somebody,

to be recognized and praised rather than to have my good deeds go unnoticed.

Given my track record for choices and what they say about me, I think I can safely predict whom I would have shouted for when Barabbas and Jesus were put up for grabs. Which has all to do with why I need a Savior.

THE CHOOSING

Given Jesus' track record He would have chosen Barabbas, or me, too. Which has everything to do with why he is the Savior.

CHAPTER SIX
THE BETRAYAL OF JACKIE

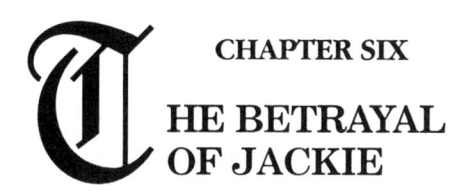

> *When thou didst say, "Seek My face," my heart said to Thee, "Thy face, O Lord, I shall seek." Do not hide Thy face from me, Do not turn Thy servant away in anger . . . Do not abandon me or forsake me, O God of my salvation.*
>
> Psalm 27:8

> *Turn to me and be gracious to me, for I am lonely and afflicted. The troubles of my heart are enlarged; bring me out of my distresses. Look upon my affliction and my trouble, and forgive all my sins.*
>
> Psalm 25:16-18

There was only one movie theater in town. It cost a dime to see the matinee on Saturday afternoon. That dime would get you a couple hours entertainment; more important yet, it would give you a wealth of vital information that could save your life. Every Saturday the kids from school were there. This was the place where you found out who was going with whom that week if you weren't in with the crowd that was privy to that kind of information. The cool people sat with their boyfriends and girlfriends. The rest of us sat in

THE LORD OF THE HUNT

groups of the same sex and observed each other's group trying to pretend they were not observing the other.

This Saturday was light turnout. "Old Yeller" was showing for two weeks. Most everybody had seen it last week, but I had missed it. Kit and Donna showed up anyway, probably just to make out in the dark; rumor had it that they had gone "all the way." Looking back I think our concept of distance was slightly off; nevertheless, they had done something that put them across the boundaries of movie house hand holding and stolen kisses. Bob and Barbara showed up, and Paul was now with Janie, Kit's old girl.

I hung around the candy counter trying to look like I was trying to make up my mind what I wanted while I kept an eye on the door to see if anyone else, a "single" person I knew, would show up. There are few things worse than seeing a good, sad movie by yourself unless you want to be by yourself. And I didn't; not particularly. Then I saw her. Jackie Burger. She was paying her dime and tip-toeing, looking through the glass ticket booth to see who was hanging out in the lobby. I waved. She waved back.

Jackie Burger. Jackie was as plain as white bread. Not ugly by gradeschool standards, just ordinary. Like most of us were. Jackie "Boogers" we called her. "Boogers" for short. I think the name originated one day at lunch when she was seen picking her nose. She suffered greatly at recess that day for her social of-

THE BETRAYAL OF JACKIE

fense and the name stuck ever since. She bore it with a blue steel gaze, never lashing out, never crying, never tattling. I'd seen many others crumble, – I'd crumbled – under far less persecution.

Jackie was by herself. I was by myself. So we sat together, more by default than by agreement since neither of us had the nerve to come to such an agreement. We sat toward the front because we were there to see the movie. The others sat in the back because they were there for other, more brave activities.

"Old Yeller" did to Jackie what it does to just about everyone who sees it. Steely and tough as I thought she was, Boogers started to cry. I wasn't exactly dry-eyed myself. Somehow our arms ended up on the armrest and neither of us made an effort to move. And so we sat, both afraid of looking at each other and both knowing what the other was feeling. Two worlds, parallel, touching but both afraid of entering the other. We left the theater having shared something wordless together and knowing something about one another that would not allow us to see one another as just "Robinson" and "Boogers" again.

Monday morning at school we did not acknowledge one another publicly. A wordless agreement that there would be no visible signs of our moment to the casual observer. I did catch her eye, often, and there was a softer, less steely look in it for me that I liked.

At lunch I sat closer to her but not with her. Unfortunately I sat close enough that Pat Grady noticed I'd closed some distance between me and Jackie.

"Hey, Robinson! Who was that you were sitting with at "Old Yeller" Saturday, huh?" Pat shouted across the lunchroom. "Wasn't that you with Boogers?"

I was nailed. "I don't know what you're talking about!" I half shouted with a quiver of fear at my impending social doom in my voice.

"Yeah you do. Robinson and Boogers were holding hands at 'Old Yeller'. I SAW you, Robinson," Pat announced to the whole lunchroom with a sing-song edge of ridicule in his voice. "Robinson li-ikes Boo-gers . . . Robinson li-ikes Boo-gers," he sang. An accompaniment of laughter filled the room.

I exploded from my seat, livid. I screamed, "I do not! I do not! I hate her. She sat by me. . . ." I stumbled for something more convincing. I looked around at the mocking faces, their mouths all gaping holes filled with obscene laughter. And I saw Jackie. She sat, still, staring at me. Her steel blue eyes were full of tears.

I bolted from the lunchroom. Tears flowed down my cheeks, tears of helpless anger, but mostly tears of something I did not understand, tears that had more to do with the way Jackie looked at me than with my frustration at Pat's orchestration of mockery. In my attempt to save myself I knew I had destroyed something precious somehow. I had violated some law within. I had desecrated a holy place I did not know existed until that moment.

I have desecrated several holy places in my life over the years, relationships I have shared with precious people. The holiness of relationships is wrought by entrusting our most private thoughts and secret feelings, and our hidden experiences to another. The unspoken law of relationships says, "You will keep my holy things as your own, you will guard them with your life, lay it down for them if need be." But we do not. We will deny our lovers and betray our friends to save our own skins. We will throw what is holy to the dogs in an unthinking heartbeat if it will preserve or benefit ourselves.

I first denied Jackie to save my sixth grade respectability, status and pride. I've betrayed and denied many others since for even less. Put the screws to me and I know I would, I have, betrayed even Christ. I have, like Judas and Peter, denied the Son of God, my friend, a love above all loves.

Though it is not told I imagine Jesus looking at Judas as he approached him in the garden to betray him. As Judas drew back from his kiss he opened his eyes to look one last time into the face of Jesus. I see Judas and Jesus suspended in a timeless moment, the sounds of rattling armor, the shouting, Malchus' whimpering all faded to nothing. There was, for that solitary moment, that look. And Judas was swallowed by a darkness as deep as death.

When Peter had denied Jesus for the third time Luke says, "And the Lord turned and looked at Peter" (Luke 22:61). Jesus was taken away. Peter went out and wept. Judas went out and died of remorse by his own hand.

Yes, Peter, yes, Judas, I understand. I have seen the look of Jesus. And I, too, have gone out and wept bitterly because in my weakness I denied all that was so precious to me. I have felt hopelessly lost because I desecrated holy trusts. I have died within because I betrayed an innocent lover to save myself.

I know the look. It was not "I told you so." It was not "You really blew it this time." It was not "You jerk, look how you've hurt me." It was not "I hate you." Those are devastating looks. I've seen them all. And they hurt because they are true, we know we deserve them.

The look Peter saw, and Judas probably saw as he kissed Jesus, was the same look I saw in the lunchroom that day. It is a look hardest of all to take, the most devastating, the hardest of all to accept because we don't deserve it. It leaves us with no way to redeem ourselves and no illusions about ourselves and where we stand with the one betrayed. It will kill us and, if we will accept its truth, it will raise us from the dead.

THE BETRAYAL OF JACKIE

It was the gospel in Jackie's tears and in the eyes of Christ. It was the look of grace; a wounded lover, eyes filled with tears, still in love with one who knows now beyond a doubt how undeserving of that love he truly is.

CHAPTER SEVEN
THE CRUCIFIXION OF LESLIE

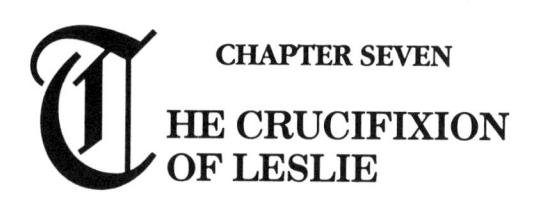

Leslie was different.

It was recess. The cool guys, as usual, sat together on the smooth granite picnic tables, their feet on the benches, their legs spread wide, elbows on their knees, hands folded in the center, all bent over, spitting conspicuously, perched like vultures judging the playground proceedings and its participants.

Leslie seldom played with anyone except me and a

couple of other uncool people.

The cool guys took counsel together, descended from their perch, circled the playground and surrounded Leslie.

Leslie was not particularly ugly, nor dimwitted, nor loud, nor arrogant, nor given to socially offensive outbursts of any kind. Leslie was just . . . different.

The cool guys began to taunt Leslie. Leslie would be their recess' entertainment today. A small crowd of fifth grade sharks, smelling blood, began gathering around them. I went, too.

Leslie was weak. Leslie wore a perpetual shroud of fearfulness. One could sense Leslie's vulnerability. Leslie never sought acceptance from the cool guys but just to be left alone.

Leslie was a boy. A tall, big boy, bigger than any of the cool guys. But he stood in their midst, his eyes bulging with fear, his arms stiff at his side, consciously, for if he did not keep them there by his will I am sure he would have hugged himself and looked even weaker than everyone suspected he was. I watched, entranced with revulsion, as the vultures picked at his fragile, silent, staring carcass.

I heard my name. And again, my name. "Yeah. Robinson!" and K. C. (I never knew what "K.C." stood for, King Cool, everyone thought), summoned me into the circle. I took a place along the edge of the circle to avoid the obvious implication of being in the middle of the circle with Leslie. "Robinson, we're gonna see who's a bigger wimp, you or Leslie. You guys are gonna fight."

I'd never been in a fight in my life. Fighting was against the school rules; it brought swift and sure wrath from the Mother Superior. I feared the crack of the ruler across my knuckles. I feared my parents finding out I was suspended for fighting. I feared my father's belt. I feared the Goliath, Leslie before me. I feared the vultures if I refused to fight, who would surely pick my carcass at the next recess.

But the thing I feared most of all was being a bigger wimp than Leslie in the eyes of all of fifth grade. I feared losing my place in the social strata. If I did not fight my place would be taken by Leslie and I would be in his. On the other hand, if I fought with unexpected viciousness and won I would gain perhaps some respect and a new, higher position in the social order.

I looked at Leslie. He stood motionless, his arms still stiff at his sides. I looked in his eyes and had to look away. I breathed a deep breath, I put my head down and I ran at Leslie like a charging bull, and tackled him. We both fell, crunching, rolling on the gravel, the circle of onlookers moving like an amoeba around us. They began cheering. They began cheering for me. Me. They were cheering for me.

THE LORD OF THE HUNT

And blind with fifth grade fear and ambition I beat Leslie. I climbed on top of his chest, closed my eyes and flailed wildly at him with all my skinny might. I closed my eyes because beneath it all I was sick. I could not look at the one suffering at my own hands, for my ambition, because of my fear. The taste of victory was vile.

Even so, when they pulled me off him I got up amid their cheers at my victory and I smiled at them. Yes, I had won in their eyes. I won their approval, I revelled in the backslapping and "way-to-go's." I walked away from Leslie, not looking back for fear someone might see an apology in my face, a look of pity or sorrow, the look of remorse I knew I could not hide if I turned. I was with THEM now. I was like them. God, I had become one of them.

Yes, God, even now, I am still one of them. Though I don't believe I'll ever again physically assault another human being, I've done and will do worse for the same motives. I am one willing to sacrifice another human being's reputation, dignity and feelings to save my place and my status. I am one willing to beat another down that I might be lifted up. I am one who walks away, oblivious to the ones I leave behind bleeding because of my self-centered actions. I am one willing to cut another down with fists of words so that he does not rise above me. I am one who feels pity, remorse, sorrow and shame but chooses the moment of bitter victory and momentary hollow acceptance over being compassionate and merciful.

Yes, I am one of them. My fifth grade sin against Leslie is the very same sin that led the Pharisees to crucify Christ. It was their fear of losing their status and their ambition to preserve the nation that sustained their high places that led them to take the Son of God up a hill and kill him (John 11:47-50).

Yes, I am one of them. As I nailed Leslie to the ground that day, and as I have nailed so many since then to save myself, I was nailing the Son of God to his cross.

I don't know if Leslie ever forgave me. I had become one of them and he left the school before I ever got the stomach to look him in the eye again.

Over the years I came to know what it meant to be one of them. It meant what I did to Leslie and the others I did to Jesus. Only this time I finally got up the guts to turn and look Jesus in the eye. My only hope is to believe that the One I nailed up two thousand years ago truly has the power to speak for everyone I've nailed up. You see, when I turned to looked at him, I heard him say, "Father, forgive them. . . . "

CHAPTER EIGHT
THE ELECTION

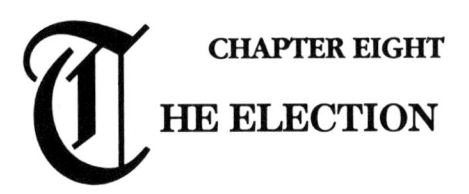

> *If I had not come and spoken to them, they would not have sin, but now they have no excuse for their sin.*
>
> John 15:22

> *The world hates me because I testify of it, that its deeds are evil.*
>
> John 7:7

> *. . . and you shall know the truth and the truth shall make you free.*
>
> John 8:32

William Chen. He was my friend and I hated him. It was because William was my friend that I hated him.

Seventh grade. We were stationed in Taiwan. I attended the parochial school because the strict discipline and tough academics were notorious there.

The Beach Boys (their first time around) were cool. Straight blond hair was in. Beatle boots and pegged pants were still in. I.D. bracelets and initials for names were in. T.J. was a guy who had it all – blond hair, bracelet, black pointed-toed boots with zippers on the sides. T.J. got to bring his lunch in a brown bag instead of a cartoon lunch box. T.J. was so cool he went steady. He actually walked with his arm draped over his girl's shoulder at school right in front of the nuns. The coolest thing of all was when he cried when he heard one of the Beach Boys lost his voice. Real tears he cried, blubbering sobs, and no one, but no one made fun of him. T.J. had it all. K.C. was almost as cool. He had dark hair but his parents let him wear it like the Beatles and he had his pants pegged.

It was not a very easy thing to be cool at Saint Vincent's. The uniform was white shirt, dark blue pants purchased from an approved tailor, white socks and black shoes. The Dominican nuns were not given to admiring coolness. The cool guys always seemed to get away with being cool while the rest of us lived in fear of being told to get our hair cut or to go to the office to change into a set of ragged, one-size-fits-all clothes they kept in there to humiliate dress code violators.

William Chen was not a cool guy. Neither was I, for that matter. But William was goofy. He laughed like a chicken. He walked like a half-sprung pogo stick. He stood too close when he talked to people, maybe because he couldn't see despite the slab of glasses that hung precariously on the end of his nose. His shirt tail hung out on one side. One sock was always at half mast. William was the Black Plague on whomever's social life he invaded; you were a dead man if you were infected with his presence. William was so goofy he wasn't even pitied. William was not cool. William was my friend.

It was not that I solicited his friendship, you understand. I guess I looked vulnerable and he simply fell in step with me one day on the way to recess and I never seemed to be able to ditch him. Perhaps I could have tried harder but I didn't have the nerve that the cool guys had when it came to William. So it was William and I, with our own table at lunch, last ones picked at P.E., science partners, and bus rides home. I didn't particularly hate him then. But I didn't enjoy him, either. Not him specifically; I got used to his chicken cackles and quirkiness. I didn't enjoy what his presence implied about me. You know, birds of a feather. Maybe it was that I was goofy, too. Maybe I was just one rung up on the ladder from him and had gotten social pity that I had always mistaken for acceptance. It was beyond terror to think maybe William was my only true friend.

It came the season for class officer elections at Saint Vincent's. Before I tell you about the meaning of the election, I must spend a moment explaining the sociology of and the procedure governing the elections.

First the sociology. Everyone knew class officer elections had both everything and nothing to do with the cool guys. It was just innately understood that the cool guys were too cool to be class officers. Thus they never got nominated and got no votes. But they voted. And so did everyone else. If nominated one need not win but just get a respectable show of votes. Votes meant affirmation, votes were a pronouncement of status, votes were a witness to one's place in a pitiless society.

Now the procedure. We nominated the candidates, Sister Mary Ellen put the names on the board. We voted by raising our hands. The candidates put their heads down as the vote for their office was counted, thus they would not see how many votes they got. The Sister would write the numbers next to the names and before the candidates were allowed to raise their heads to view the results, the losing candidates' names and votes were erased so none would know how many votes they got. Of course there was nothing keeping the losers from asking their friends how many votes they got, except maybe embarrassment.

Class officer elections meant nothing more to me than a half of a morning without academics. But this morning they meant everything to me. William Chen nominated me for class president.

I was a realist. I could face the fact that I would not win against the likes of Mike Esmark or Pat Grady. Mike had been class president since fifth grade. His re-election in subsequent years was insured when he offered to take six swats from Swingin' Sister Jude so the whole class would not have to do extra homework for a week for being rowdy in the lunchroom. She gave him the swats, we did no homework and Mike was president for three years running. I had no such platform on which to run, so I knew I would not win.

I truly had no desire to win except the crazy "wouldn't it be great if" that you feel when you have no hopes. I did have a delirious desire to know the vote, an exhilarating fear and dread of knowing where I stood, William Chen notwithstanding, what my true place was, to have my existence acknowledged and affirmed by my peers, yea, even the cool guys.

And it came our turn to put our heads down, foreheads on the forearm, while our names were called and the votes were counted for president of the class.

Mike Esmark. A rustle of sleeves, a rumble of shifting postures, a long pause, chalk scuffing and tapping on the board. Double digits.

Steve Robinson. I listened, my ears acute with fear and hope, and heard nothing save a distant choked laugh from the back of the room. I could not help it; insane with dread, I opened my eyes and peeked over the top of my forearm. Though I could only see two-thirds of the class I knew what the remaining one third looked like. There grinning like a porpoise, sat William Chen. A solitary hand raised high and proud for his best friend. And I hated him.

I don't recall Pat Grady's name even being called, so consumed with hate I was, and with the single scratch of the chalk on the board roaring in my ears.

Oh, William Chen, how I hated you that day. Had you not called my name I could have lived gladly, perhaps with suspicions and dread, but blissfully, even willfully ignorant of what I truly was. Had you not called my name I would not be the object of giggling lunchroom derision and the butt of merciless playground hilarity. I would not be numbered with the lowest and least and fools. William, with your hand held high that day, solitary in your acceptance of me, you killed me, and I hated you. You were my only friend and I hated you.

But now, William, I love you for I know now you were truly a Christ to me. You were the gospel incarnate, a living word making straight the way of the Lord within me. You see, years later another came to me, one who was also despised and rejected of men. He said he came to be the friend of the last and lowest, the sinners and outcasts. Like you, William, he called my name. Mine. He called my name and I could no longer avoid knowing the dreadful truth about myself that I feared. Through him I knew what I truly was. I knew by his call that I, too, was numbered with the lowly and the fools, the rejects and the sinners. He was not cool, nor was I, but this time it mattered not to me because I did not hate him.

This one was Jesus Christ, William. His call is a call of grace. His gospel is the story of a friend like you. It is of God who took on legs of flesh and fell in step

THE ELECTION

with and, yes, fell in love with the outcasts. It is of one who was rejected by all but who will not reject any. It is of one who seeks and finds and will not be ditched by those he chooses to befriend. It is of one whose presence means our death in this world but who turns out to be the only life there is. It is of a friend who will endure our hatred of him until we learn to love.

This is of my friend who, even knowing what I truly am, called my name one day. And on that day he raised his hands, nailed high and proud, in solitary acceptance of me.

William, meet Jesus, my other friend. And I love him.

CHAPTER NINE
THE WILL OF GOD

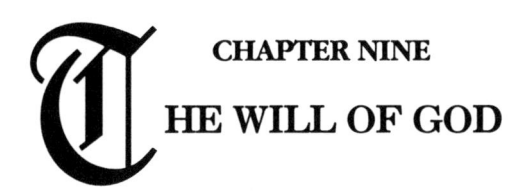

> *This is good and acceptable in the sight of God our Savior, who desires all men to be saved and to come to a knowledge of the truth.*
> *I Timothy 2:3-4*

I loved her to distraction.

That evening held us in its loom, weaving our histories together, now and forever a tapestry irrevocably bound by one look, one touch. From that moment, so pregnant with magnificent consequence, that very moment, I knew I would have her. She would be my beloved, I would be hers. And so her heart's desire became my obsession.

Oh, yes, I could name her imperfections for you. I could tell you of her weaknesses. I could reveal the hidden things of her heart, her fears, the places so dark they frightened even her. I could disclose to you the secrets in her past that still she speaks about in guarded whispers. But I will not. I loved her, I love her, and those things are of no consequence to me. My desire for her was never diminished by the discovery of her weakness and flaws. My wish to work magic in her life never changed, but grew more intense as she revealed her struggles. As I came to know her pain, my desire for her healing deepened.

I wished joy for her, unending, incredible joy that would release her from her past, her demons, her fears. I wanted her to lay her heart's burdens on me, to find solace within my arms, shelter in my love for her. I desired above all else that she seek me out as one who could bring joy into her life and was willing to take her sorrows and comfort her. I wanted her to know my life was hers, all I was and had was for her. I longed for her to find me loving her beyond her wildest imaginings, caring for her heart and soul sometimes more than she cared for them herself. I was willing to sacrifice all I had for her, joyfully, and never look back, if that would bring a smile into her wearied life.

It was my desire for her to be at peace. It was my will, my heart's deepest longing that I could see her face without the lines of sorrow and distress. Her healing became my greatest need, her rest became my burden. I would forgive anything, I would accept her in all of her guilt. I wept for the secrets she kept from even me and for her unspeakable pain. I would give her my gifts hoping she would know they were from my heart, a shadow of the offering of my life for hers. I died ten thousand times for her, wishing I knew what I could do that she would know she was wondrous and loved beyond telling.

I wanted above all else that she find her deepest longings fulfilled in me, in my love for her, in my life given for her. I was jealous, outraged when she would seek healing and comfort in another. But even in my jealousy I loved her, sometimes waited for her, sometimes pursued her. I could not reject her, I could not give up pouring out my heart to her even when she was not there to accept it. I was wounded many times and yet I bore the scars like precious jewels of outrageous cost.

I was hopelessly lost in her. I was powerless to give up my pursuit of her heart. I was joyously, wonderfully, passionately in love with her. I could only give, forgive, accept, forebear, and comfort. My desire was for her alone, my longings were for her peace and joy. My will was that she be one with me and me alone, and find within me all that she was seeking. There was no cost too high, no price too great to pay for the possession of her devotion and love.

I could not command her to love me, only pursue her. I could not direct her except by enticing her. I could not hold over her my gifts, my love or my sacrifices, only lay them before her. My will was my desire for her good. I held no power over her except as she yielded herself to the power of my love for her. I could only tell her of my dreams for her, for us. I could not coerce her to dream my dreams; I could not force her to fulfill my desires. But if she did fall in love with me I knew it would be with all of her heart, soul, mind and strength. It would then be her will, her desire, not mine. My dreams would then be her dreams. She would love me with the depth and passion that no command could force nor word from me could create.

And this is the desire of God: that all men be saved and come to a knowledge of the truth, the truth of his eternal pursuit of our love. This is the desire of God, this is his passion, his deepest longing. In the compelling power of my love I have seen only a passing shadow of the love of my God for me. My desire is but a dying distant star beside the flame of his desire. My shallow longings for my beloved are drowned in the depth of his longings for my heart and soul. I see only dimly his love in the mirror of my heart's wildest desires.

He wills that I have joy, he wills my peace. He would be my shelter, the one who would take my burdens and dry my tears. He would heal my broken heart. He lays his gifts before me, his life for mine, his heart for mine, his sorrow for my joy, his scars for my healing. He is powerless to relent in his pursuit of my love. No price was too high to consider, no cost too great to pay for my devotion.

My God, how you love me. I have come to know you love me beyond my wildest imaginings. I know I am loved beyond telling. Your desire is now mine, my beloved. You have pursued me, enticed me, and finally won me. My heart is yours. I touch the scars you so beautifully bore for me and all that is within me cries out, "He is my Beloved, and I am his."

CHAPTER TEN
THE MAN IN THE MALL

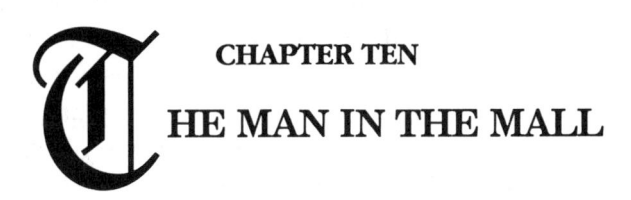

But when you give a reception, invite the poor, the crippled, the lame, the blind....

Luke 14:13

I just happened to be on that side of town. I was waiting for a contractor to cut checks and needed to kill some time, so I went to the mall for lunch. This mall was my old teen-age stomping ground. Dave and I almost wore a path in the granite floor during our senior year of high school. Mostly we watched people. Mostly girls, actually. But people in general, too.

I got a sandwich at the deli and sat down in the mall to watch people. It was then that I saw him again.

He was sitting on the edge of one of the red brick planters, like always. He had one arm crossed, resting his useless hand in his lap, the hand that swung on his arm like a knot at the end of a rope at his side when he walked. With the index finger of his other hand he traced figure eights in the dirt in the planter, like always. I would swear he wore the same black rimmed glasses with dirty lenses as thick as Fig Newtons. He still wore light blue denim bell bottoms and tennis shoes prematurely worn on one side from his shuffle-walk. His back had become even more hunched on the side of his good arm. When he looked up to watch the passers-by, (he always tilted his head way back to look up because his body was hunched forward and his glasses had slid down his nose) his head would list to one side and rest on his hump and his mouth would hang open. I watched him watch people walk by, just as I have seen him do every time I had been to that mall, just as I saw him do for the first time twenty years ago.

Twenty years. I imagined him for twenty years (maybe more, that is only the time I know of) going to the mall every day for eight or ten hours, shuffling, sitting, then shuffle some more, then sit a while longer. I wondered what he thought about while shuffling, sitting and watching for all those years. I wondered what he was capable of thinking about.

I wondered if he was ever jealous of the whole people. I wondered if he was ever angered by his ugliness, or if he perceived he is ugly. (I know, "different" would be kinder, but not as honest given our culture's love affair with beauty.)

I wondered if he ever wanted children to buy toys for, or a wife to watch try on a new dress, or if he had a wife, or children maybe before some calamity struck him down.

I wondered if he ever stifled the urge to risk saying hello (I'd never heard him speak, though) to one of the shoppers, a pretty woman, a toddling child, a blue-haired widow, a man in a wheelchair, just to hear a voice speak directly to him.

I wondered if he ever left feeling lonelier than when he arrived, and if so, how much more loneliness on top of loneliness he could bear after twenty years.

I wondered if God, in his mercy, had short circuited whatever part of his heart and mind it is that would allow him to know he was different and so alone.

I wondered, too, about all the people that pass him every day, if they even see him, if they consider who he might be, or what is going on inside him. I wondered if any of them thank God, their stars, their karma or even blind luck for not being like him.

I wondered what would happen if God in his mercy made each person who passed him like him for one day, letting them live in the twisted wreck of flesh he occupied, letting them feel his accumulated feelings, whatever they are. I wondered how life in the mall would change, how life beyond the mall would change.

I wondered how many people who have passed him in twenty years are Christians. I wondered how many of them have seen him. I wondered how many of them have stopped to talk to him. I wondered how many of them have made any attempt to see if he was hurting, to find out if his heart was broken or if he lived in desperation or in anger at our God. I wondered how many of them know what Jesus said about compassion, the last being the first, the outcast being welcomed in, the gospel being preached to the poor in pocket and spirit. I wondered why, if some seventy five percent of our nation claims to be "Christian" not one of the hundred or more people who passed this man during that hour ever stopped to acknowledge his existence, much less his obvious isolation and probable pain.

I finished my sandwich. And as I left to go pick up my checks, I wondered why I, too, did not.

CHAPTER ELEVEN
THE DERELICT

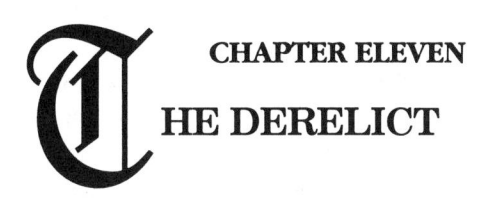

> *Do not neglect to show hospitality to strangers, for by this some have entertained angels without knowing it.*
> **Hebrews 13:2**

It was close to Christmas. I remember because of the bitter cold and my new long, black overcoat. It was Hobo Joe's Coffee Shop about 10:00 p.m. after our Wednesday night mid-week church service. I remember because Randy and I hung out there a lot in those days, righting the world's injustices, talking about God, and watching people, sometimes until dawn.

We saw a lot of severe humanity late at night. Cruis-

THE LORD OF THE HUNT

ing gays, hookers, drunks of every variety, rowdy cowboys, monosyllabic druggies, lonely businessmen and glassy-eyed insomniacs. This night there was a broken and withered man staring into an empty coffee cup, his hands shaking like crisp brown leaves in the cold winter wind. He had obviously more than taken advantage of the free refills on his one cup of coffee. The manager was at his table in a muted confrontation, his tone giving away his tune. Anyone could have named his tune in three notes.

Let me tell you a little about Randy. The thing that attracted me to him was his enormous capacity for compassion and righteous indignation, and that he would do something . . . anything, shamelessly or aggressively if he thought an injustice was being perpetrated. Situations at which most people would bite their lips and shake their heads and then go home and say, "You won't believe what I saw today . . .," Randy would DO something, and, if necessary, throw down the gauntlet before the oppressors.

We decided this situation warranted intervention. We got up and went over to the old man's table and said, "Bob! What are you doing here? How are you, old buddy? Hey, why don't you come join us, we were just getting ready to eat." The man, never looking up, slowly raised his shaking body from his table and obediently shuffled to our table, the manager matching our steps. Randy turned and said, "He's with us. We need a menu, please."

Old winos aren't long on brilliant conversation or imaginative small talk. It was a quiet meal, solemn, almost sacramental. Randy and I didn't discuss much theology that night. I guess you could say we watched it eat.

When he finished we took the old man to the County Hospital to detoxify. I gave him my winter coat because we knew he'd be back on the street in about twelve hours. We never knew what happened to him; we never got his real name. He's forever "Bob." Actually, he's eternally Jesus.

You see, "Bob" was with us for a while that night. I think in the eternal scheme of things we are like him in many ways. We are all abandoned winos (what we chose to dull our pain with is irrelevant, really), with a past full of heartaches too deep for words, seeking a little warmth, shelter for a few moments from the cold without and within. Someone came along, told the Manager, "They are with me," and gave us his body and blood to eat. Randy and I just passed the free meal on to another lonely, hungry wino that night.

"I was hungry and you gave me food, I was thirsty and you gave me drink, I was a stranger and you welcomed me, I was naked and you clothed me. . . . Truly I say to you, as you did it to one of the least of these my brethren, you did it to me" (Matthew 25:35-46).

1970'S
PART THREE

GOD IS LOVE...

CHAPTER TWELVE
I WAS BLIND BUT NOW I SEE

Rick was probably just born about the time Harry anointed me with the gift of vision. Rick is nineteen and works for me. He has a young mind; it is set on the Spirit.

Harry was a crazy heart of compassion. I fell in love with him at first sight.

Harry had a story to tell that he told with a pure heart. It was story that began with rock and roll bands and heroin addiction. In the middle was throwing rocks from across the street at the church where his brother preached. At the end was a couple with faith that took him in as a wasted, hopeless addict. They said, "Harry, make yourself at home. We're going out. There's the refrigerator, help yourself to whatever you want." Instead of coming home to a house stripped to nakedness for a fix, they came home to Harry scrubbing their kitchen floor on his hands and knees.

There was no spiritual oneupmanship in his story. No aftertaste of pride in his depths of sin. It was that Harry was saved, introduced to his Savior Jesus by two people with faith. He told of it purely.

Harry was a man of God who painted houses. The second time I went to Abilene to see him, the note on his door said he was painting a house, come on over. I went to the address and drove into the dirt along the side of the house. I reached for my key to turn off the motor and "Bang!"

"Get out of there! I said get out! You'll kill my grass, get out, get out!" The screen door flew open, "Bang!" against the side of the house next door, and an old woman with a face like a walnut powdered white, waving a broom, waddling like an angry goose burst out the door screaming. "Get out of there!"

I ducked down to look up through the windshield at Harry on his ladder and he waved me to back up and go around the other side of the house. I looked at the old woman and with the appropriate edge of sarcasm in my voice said, "Sor-ry," as I backed up. She looked long enough to be sure I was going away and went back to her house exhausted from the battle.

I parked. Harry and I exchanged hugs and I said, "Man, what's with her?"

Harry smiled at me. "Oh, Mrs. Smith? She's just lonely. Let's paint."

Harry had eyes to see and ears to hear. He had a heart crazy with compassion for a whole world of lonely souls. With one sentence Harry had taught me to see. I never saw the world the same after that. Ever. At different times I've blessed and cursed him for opening my eyes.

Rick was new with my company and we were working together remodeling a patient's wing of a hospital. There was an old man on the job who poured concrete floors. He was bony and had a disposition like flint; sparks flew whenever someone came in contact with him. People nonchalantly slipped into a convenient room and hid when he came down the corridors. The old man came in the room where we were working. It was a small room and he could not be avoided, so we tried to look lost in our task at hand. It didn't work.

"Yeah, these hospitals think they got all the latest gadgets. Bull. The Russians and Japanese been having this stuff for years."

At times like that I automatically slip into my counselor's non-judgmental response mode. "You don't say." I kept my face to the wall, trying to look like I was concentrating. Rick was concentrating on my face to figure out what his face should look like.

"Yeah, we only think we got the world beat out in technology. In Yugoslavia they. . . ." I don't remember anything of what he said after that, his stream of consciousness overflowed the banks of my comprehension. I turned away from the wall to face the human being before me. I listened. Rick fidgeted, leaned against the wall, head down, now head back and mouth open with boredom, shuffle of feet, long sigh. Twenty minutes later the old man stopped. Abruptly.

"Better get back to work. See ya."

"Yeah, us too. See ya." I turned and Rick was staring at me.

"Steve." Rick always paused long between my name and his next sentence in situations like this. "What was that all about?"

"Rick." I paused too. "That was about an old man who is very lonely."

"Oh."

And I knew from the look on Rick's face that his eyes were opened.

We went back to work. I smiled to myself at the thought of Harry's gift being passed on yet again in another twenty years, to one just being born, whose eyes are closed tight to the world.

CHAPTER THIRTEEN

SECOND HAND PEOPLE, THRIFT STORE CHURCHES

> *... you were not redeemed with perishable things like silver and gold from your futile way of life inherited from your forefathers, but with precious blood, as of a lamb unblemished and spotless, the blood of Christ.*
> *I Peter 1:18–19*
>
> *Blessed are the poor in spirit, for theirs is the kingdom of heaven.*
> *Matthew 5:3*
>
> *Thy kingdom come, thy will be done on earth as it is in heaven.*
> *Matthew 6:10*

Name Brand Closeouts 40-50% Off!

Factory to You!

Designer Seconds, Blems, 60% Below Retail!

I admit it. I'm far from poor and I don't have to, but I shop the thrift stores, the swap meets, the discount warehouses, the factory outlets. I love the tables piled high with a thousand out of style belts, shoes dumped three feet deep in a bin with laces tied together so the pairs won't get separated, seeing what was hot just three months ago now piled ignominiously on a folding table with four red slashes through the price tag. It is a challenge to find the minute flaw that inspector number 312 (whose "fortune cookie slip" is still in the pocket) found that caused him to consign the garment to the reject rack.

It is a grim reality, the reject rack. In our automated, sophisticated, technologically perfected world there are still rejects. That is why there are the seconds outlets. But then there are the thrift stores. Thrift stores are the warehouses for the really undesirable, the used up and worn out, the way out of fashion, the unwanted, the stuff that cannot command even a discount price any longer because it is fatally flawed.

It is kind of a sad thing to me that the notion of "thrift stores" has been elevated to vogue and respectable establishments where people in Guess jeans and Vuarnet sunglasses can shop comfortably. When I first began "slumming," the thrift stores were all in the part of downtown where you took your life in your hands if you shopped there looking like you didn't need to shop there. Only the second hand people bought second hand merchandise. But times have changed. Merchandisers have capitalized on an idea that used to meet needs and now serves wants.

Just as the times have changed so has the church

changed, which is a thing of greater sadness to me. I just don't think what we have is what Jesus had in mind when he came and set up his establishment. When the word became flesh he fashioned his humanity in the tacky, the common, the crude. He came not as a "designer human" but as last year's lapels, cheap polyester, and wide ties. He was not the statement of what's fashionably hot in religion: the charcoal gray pinstripe with understated pleats of fasting, abstinence, good company, piety, holy walk and talk, and halos. He came in the hopelessly tacky leisure suit of eating and drinking, laughing and joking with the fast crowd, walking where common feet walked, straight-talking the common talk, and bathing about as often as a fisherman. Nicodemus probably had to swat flies the whole time he talked with Jesus.

When Jesus came slumming in the flesh, he shopped the thrift stores of humanity. He searched the human reject racks, the seconds warehouses. He found the unfashionable lepers, the worn-out divorcees, the shop-worn prostitutes, the broken demoniac, the unwanted con-men and tax collectors, the flawed man with the short-circuited epileptic son, the less than perfect fishermen, the undesirable blind, lame, and dying, the less than whole paraplegic, in short, the whole mess of flawed human seconds and rejects. These were the ones discounted by "religion," rejected by the holy inspectors, cast aside as useless and worthless by those in vogue and in touch with the latest religious fashion statements issued by the Calvin Klein's and Armani's of piety and righteousness.

He viewed as a secondhand Messiah saving secondhand humanity, and he took his life in his hands when he did it. And it was his very life that he offered up for the discounted, useless, worthless, irreparable, and cast-offs. He deemed priceless what others threw away. He considered precious what others found worthless. He loved what others had come to despise.

Yes, times have changed. Jesus' church is no longer seen as a seedy place downtown for the rejected, the exceedingly common, the broken, the flawed, the useless. We are not the true thrift store of humanity that Jesus established. We are now glitzy designer outlets, dealing with only slightly blemished versions of that which is fashionable and acceptable. Sometimes you really have to hunt for the flaws.

Designer people can shop comfortably in the church now. There is little risk, no chance they'll get stuck with something really out of date and undesirable. We've opened outlets uptown and in the malls, we've franchised acceptability, neon, polished floors, lots of parking, wide aisles, climate-controlled comfort, and mass marketing. The church is clinically clean, disinfected, spotless, and polished. No one has to swat flies in our assemblies. Our facades keep most of the undesirable elements out, since they know they don't have what it takes to buy what we are selling anyway. They may come in but it's mostly to window shop because they know they cannot afford us. But just in case, we have our Security Measures (the subtle snubs, sideways glances, and keeping them out of public view – when was the last time a ragman served at your communion table?) to be sure the riff-raff doesn't hang around long and upset the carefully contrived ambiance of our assemblies.

I miss the old thrift stores, the excitement of finding priceless treasures cast off by someone who knew not the value of oddball things. I miss the old kingdom where the unwanted are precious, where no price is too high to pay for the worthless, where no one is discounted because of flaws. I miss the flies, the smell of mothballs and mildew, the risk of getting dirty, the ragged informality, and the idea that the poor in spirit (and pocket) don't feel we're selling something they cannot afford.

I cannot help but wonder what we would do if, when we prayed, "Thy kingdom come," it did come into our midst, fully, in all its vulgar glory and inelegant holiness of blemished humanity redeemed by the precious blood of Christ.

Perhaps we'd better watch how we pray.

CHAPTER FOURTEEN
THE LORD OF THE HUNT

My father is what you would call a "good ol' boy" from Arkansas. The kind of guy Paul meant in Romans 5:7 when he said "for a good man someone would die." The "give you the shirt off his back" kind of guy. And he has several friends, also good old boys, that he goes hunting with every year. I have gone with them a few times and over the years I began to notice a certain pattern of behavior, a ritual, if you will, that occurs between the hunting seasons.

THE LORD OF THE HUNT

This is how it goes. They will all get together on a Saturday or Sunday afternoon and have a couple beers, fix a few steaks or burgers, and sit around the living room and tell old hunting stories. That in itself though, does not qualify to be elevated to ritual status. This is where it becomes ritual: they tell the same stories over and over to one another knowing full well they were all there and all participated in and witnessed the events. Even so, they all still guffaw at the time Tom's tent flooded, and groan at the time the trophy buck got away when Bob's gun misfired, and lament the time they walked four days in the slog and muck and saw nothing. They were all there, they all know the stories, they all know the punch lines, the surprise endings, (they even know the lies), yet they tell the stories as though it were yesterday, as to strangers, laughing and crying as though the tales were being told for the first time in their hearing. The old stories never grow old, the number of times they are told never seems to quench the sincerity of the laughter, the earnestness, the intensity of the telling. And I honestly believe it never will.

And these are some of Jesus' old hunting stories.

There was a sheep that wandered off and the shepherd, instead of being a good chief financial officer and writing off the one percent as an operating loss, jeopardizes his whole enterprise and sets off to hunt for the wayward one (Luke 15:3-7).

There were two children of God who, when they

had disobeyed, like most little children, hid under the bed when they heard their Father walk in the door. The Father called out to them, "Where are you?" and ever since has been looking behind the couches, under the beds and inside the closets for his precious, disobedient children, calling out to them "Where are you?" (Genesis 3:1-11, Luke 15:8-10).

And my favorite. God invited some rich and snooty people to a party that would end all parties and they sent flimsy regrets, turning him down flat. So he sent his servants out to hunt up some guests because he had this lavish spread sitting drawing flies, and he was going to have his party come hell or high water. (Actually, both had come but neither ultimately threw a wet blanket on his plans for the party.) He sent the servants downtown to the shelters and the alleyways, the halfway houses and the whore houses, the bars and the motels, and said, "Hunt up the bag-ladies, the winos, the crazies and lazies, the wild-eyed, the shopping cart people, the smelly, the ragged, the hopeless, the helpless, the fearful, the wasted, and tell them they are the guests of honor at the king's party." They came, they found out there is such a thing as a free lunch, and a good time was had by all (Luke 14:15-24).

And these hunting stories, my friends, are what the Lord's Supper is all about. It is a time when we get together with our closest friends, share a great old bottle of wine (or Welch's) and some bread, and tell each other the same old stories about the hunt. And like all true stories that become ritual among friends, time

THE LORD OF THE HUNT

and repetition do not diminish the earnestness nor the intensity of the telling, nor does it dull the hearing and feelings.

Sure, we've heard the hunting stories a thousand times. We were all there, we all know the surprise ending, but we all still laugh and cry at the punch line: Jesus died for you. Jesus died for me. I was lost, but now I'm found.

CHAPTER FIFTEEN
REMEMBER ME

I gave the offense in my first year as a minister. I remember my very words, I remember the crushing result, I remember the hurt, I remember my attempt at an apology that was more horrible than the insult itself. I couldn't help but remember; I saw him every week and I knew (no, I suspected) he remembered it all, too.

My Sunday school class met in the old education building that smelled of old wood and damp brick. It was a maze of wide, white corridors and numberless rooms. One Sunday morning a poster appeared, thumbtacked onto the door of the room where I taught. It proclaimed "The Fruit of the Spirit" lettered in bright, dayglo colors. Love. Joy. Peace. Patience. Kindness. Goodness. Gentleness. Self-control. It was not "art" but I was flattered. I took it to mean that someone actually saw those qualities in my life.

As it turned out whoever it was that made the poster left off of the list a quality of my life not generated by the Spirit: Stupidity.

After a year I was finally allowed to conduct the most prestigious and important part of our Sunday morning assembly: Making announcements. Only the elder statesmen of the church with either power or charm got to make announcements. I deduced I had charmed the one in charge of making the assignment. I stepped into the pulpit. I smiled. I greeted our visitors with warmth and sincerity. I compassionately read the names of our sick and bereaved. I announced our upcoming events with enthusiasm. Finally I told about our Sunday school classes. I indicated all the classes by their room numbers or relative positions in the building. North-west corner, south-west corner, north-east corner. Except mine. I said we met in the room with the ugly poster on the door.

If the pulpit had burst into flames and consumed me it would have been a merciful fate. I hoped I was really home in bed just awakening from a horrible dream. I hoped against hope that two hundred people simultaneously went momentarily deaf. Or that whoever made the poster was not there by some fluke of God's merciful providence.

But none of those things happened. I was still there, wide awake after the closing song. They all heard it. Whoever made the poster was there. It was gone the next Sunday. I don't really know that anyone noticed it was gone but me.

I was discreetly told (as discreetly as can be told in a small country church) who made the poster for me. It was Old Uncle Will, whom I loved, and who loved me. The poster moved from the category of "meaningful" to me into the realm of "precious." And my insult went from "dumb" to "heinous." I could not fathom he could forgive me so I mailed him an apology which really wasn't an apology. Rather than admit the utter wretchedness of my act, I tried to lighten the seriousness of the offense by passing it off lightly between some glib small talk in a hasty note. I dropped the letter into the mouth of the mailbox and as it burped a hollow "thunk" I wished I could retrieve it and begin again. Mail, like words, is irretrievable.

I never had the guts to talk to him face to face to apologize for the remark and for the apology. So every Sunday and Wednesday for years I suffered for my cowardice and searched his face for some kind of look (what it would look like I never have figured out) that would tell me all is forgiven and forgotten. Knowing him, the look was there all along, I just did not allow myself to see it.

For some reason I could never forget my words. I could never forget the hurt I imagined I inflicted on that gracious gentleman. I have always hoped he has long forgotten what I did. Partly for him, but more for me. I needed to know or feel or learn that I was forgiven, that the quality within me that would make me say something so stupid, callous and hurtful has been forgotten by him.

It may seem to you much agony over a slip of the tongue, so small an offense. "Just forget it," I was advised by a deacon of the church when I asked him what I should do after I made the offending remark. But I couldn't. And I cannot still. And I tell you the truth, I have other more terrible things I have inflicted on people that I wish I could forget. (Not that I lie awake and neurotically ruminate over them, but at odd times they sneak up on me and twist my innards.)

I will take a wild stab in the dark and say there are probably things you have said and done that, now and then, you agonize over still though it is now years later. The irretrievable cutting words and callous actions. You know you should just forget it, but you know you never will, and you can only wish and hope everyone else has.

Life is very much a weaving of relationships that influence us by how others remember us and sometimes whether they remember us. There are times when we die if we are not remembered. There are times we wish we could die (perhaps not literally, but at least disappear, become nonexistent) when we know how we are remembered. We know well the power remembrance holds over us.

The hope that we are remembered.

The emptiness of being forgotten.

The wish that someone would forget.

The joy of being remembered.

There was a time in the early sixties, I have forgotten exactly when, that the phrase "Forget you!" was a popular put down. Though I do not recall any of us at Dodson Junior High having any conscious intentions of inflicting an existential crisis on our classmates by hurling the phrase at them, perhaps even as junior high students we understood our deep need to be remembered by someone, somewhere, somehow, that assures us of our significance in a world that is given to forgetting who we are, that we are worthwhile, that we even exist.

As I have grown up I have been forgotten, and died within for it. I have been remembered and rejoiced for it. I have been remembered and wished I could edit the memories, or wipe them out of the mind of the rememberer. Some of my strongest feelings come from remembering certain people. I am sure the remembrance of me brings strong feelings to others, some joyful, some sad, some mad. Like most people I have not always lived in a way that people will remember me in the way I would like to be remembered when I am dead.

I think at the root of all this anxiety over being remembered and being forgotten has to do with our value, our worth, the significance of our very existence in an amnesiac universe that seems to ultimately value no one, and whose only equity is that the significant and insignificant, the worthless and worthy (by any measure of those things) finally and ultimately end up the same.

And this is the significance of the cross of Jesus Christ flanked by two very forgettable men with lives full of unforgettable offenses. The Worthy Significant One and two worthless insignificant ones all dying one death, all about to be snuffed out because the world wanted to forget that they all existed.

The cry of the thief on the cross is, in my mind, the most pitiable cry Jesus heard in his whole ministry. Consider the thief. He had no hope for forgiveness, no hope for rescue, no hope for another chance to reform, much less to prove he could reform, no hope for pardon, his life was the price for his crime. He was facing death and the oblivion of non-existence. In a few hours he would be gone and eventually he would be forgotten, though the pain he inflicted on others would probably be remembered.

"Remember me . . . ," he asked, as though if he only existed in the mind of Jesus somewhere, somehow, that would be enough to keep him from oblivion.

"Remember me . . ." he asked. Not, "Remember ABOUT me."

"Remember ME."

What could Jesus take to eternity ABOUT the thief? That he was a thief, a repeat offender, a thug, a punk, a violator of other's rights and property, a blight on society, unreformable, incorrigible, a big-time loser, one deemed by the world that the world would be a better place if he no longer existed, a worthless reprobate and hopeless case.

"Do not remember ABOUT me. Remember ME. Please, forget ABOUT me, Jesus." That is the cry of hope against hope, the most desperate of all requests in the Scriptures and in our own lives. When nothing about us seems salvageable, redeemable, or restorable, we are out of time, strength, and even faith, when we find ourselves hopelessly entangled in sin and its consequences, we can only hope, we do hope, that we will just be remembered. Isn't this our deepest hope, (the one we feel so sharply when we realize someone has forgotten us), that we will just be remembered? At the same time there is the hope that all that there is ABOUT us, our darkness, our failure, our weakness, and our transgressions are forgotten. To be remembered, just remembered, is to know somehow that we exist, we are significant, we matter, we are worth remembering in spite of it all. We want to know with certainty that somewhere, somehow, contrary to the economy of the universe, the fact we just exist is important, more important than even what we are doing or have done with our existence.

This is what Jesus promises us in the gospel, that because of his cross he can and does forget ABOUT us and simply remembers us. In the economy of the gospel no THINGS are remembered but no ONE is forgotten simply because he deems us worth remembering.

The backwards economy of the gospel also discounts another kind of remembering. It discounts the human desire to be remembered for the good we have done. "To the one who does not expect to be paid for his ledger full of good works but believes in him who gives life to the one with a debit column full of ungodliness, his faith is credited as righteousness," Paul says (Romans 4:5 paraphrased). In judgment there will be the ones who will demand that Jesus remember all the good things about them. They will say, "Lord, Lord, remember us? Please allow us to refresh your memory about all the good things we did for you, how we prophesied in your name, and cast out demons in your name and did so many wonderful pious religious activities for you." The Lord will answer them, "I'm sorry, not only do I not recall those things, your face doesn't ring a bell either" (Matthew 7:21ff, paraphrased).

You see, the message of the gospel is this: God has a very short list of things he remembers. He remembers his Son's death on the cross. He remembers us. Other than that he draws a blank. He doesn't get to know us except by a personal introduction. All we need to do as we are hanging out in this world dying in our sin, is look to Jesus dying for our sin, and introduce ourselves to him with our last and most desperate gasp of breath.

And he never forgets a name.

CHAPTER SIXTEEN
How I Am

> *Wretched man that I am! Who will set me free from this body of death?*
> Romans 7:24

> *Who will bring a charge against God's elect? God is the one who justifies....*
> Romans 8:33

If they had put up a marquee in front of the boys' home:

Double Feature! Now Showing:

Love
and
Compassion

starring Steve Robinson
as Counselor of Children

I might have been a little embarrassed at the barefaced egotism of it. But if it was also in lights I wouldn't have been that much more embarrassed.

The boys' home was a treatment facility where the state placed severely emotionally disturbed kids that could not make it in foster homes or other institutions. My wife and I lived with eight of them in a large, old turquoise-green house set in the middle of twenty-four isolated desert acres that had dead, rusted-out farm machinery lying about it.

I had just graduated with my bachelor's degree in ministry and needed a mission to fulfill. Salvaging the home (physically and programatically) and the boys (emotionally and spiritually) was perfect. It was taking on a hopeless cause (which I always enjoy doing) and it was James' "pure and undefiled religion," taking care of emotional orphans in their affliction. We accepted the job with the home, after much prayer, sincerely. As usual, my pride found a home, too.

Yes, as it turned out, there were unlimited opportunities for my ego in these unwanted children. I would want them, I would love them, I would find a way, through the love of Christ, to take care of them, get through to them, and change their hearts and minds. Yes, I would do that for them. And for me.

You see, the thing I liked most about being at the home was that it fit my image of myself: patient, wise, spiritual, kind, compassionate and selfless. In brazen shorthand, "savior." I enjoyed, no, I arrogantly delighted in the idea that we took on a job and were taking kids that no one else wanted or could handle. And I took liberties to set up opportunities to let people know that's what we did. When people were duly impressed, I smiled and accepted their praise as humbly as I could muster.

We were there for only three weeks and already I loved all the boys. Every one. Except John Gaston.

John was a small, wiry kid who came from an abusive family. He had hair like shredded wheat and looked mean and dirty even in Mickey Mouse PJ's at bedtime. Johnny's face had a perpetual look that, if he were in the group of kids brought to Jesus, even Jesus, I think, would want to slap it off. People who met Johnny hated him in seconds flat. He set land speed records for setting distance between himself and other human beings. All the kids hated him. The other staff people hated him. I, on the other hand, hated the sin but loved the sinner. So I said. Actually, I hated him, too.

I knew all the correct ways to view his behavior. The cry for help behind the foul abusive attacks, the "I'll get you to reject me so I don't get involved and hurt again" syndrome, the frightened child inside the macho bravado, the tender heart beneath the crusty scabs and scars of abuse. And I knew the correct way to view myself. I was the expert, the one with knowledge, wisdom and the answers. But I was also, on top of all that, one with the compassion of Christ in my heart. I had love, agape, the love for the undeserving, unlovely, the outcast and hopeless cases. I was spiritual, yes, and more so than those before me who gave up on him. I would break through to this child with love, tough love, unrelenting spiritual love, I knew I would, I knew I must. For him. And for me.

Johnny would not have it. Actually it was more like he would not let ME have it, that is, my precious view of myself. With him I could not be who I believed I was. And I think I hated him for that more than anything else. He would bait me and I could not be compassionate. I could not be patient and wise. I could not even be objective, detached and professional. I wanted to slap him. I wanted to take him to the woodshed and thrash him. But the state law said no woodshed thrashings. No physical punishment. But he needed it. For his good. And for mine.

The seven who came to the office door were missing only a rope to qualify as a lynch mob. Johnny had gone in their rooms and trashed, deliberately and precisely, favorite possessions of each boy. Posters, toys, clothing, and sports equipment all cut up, smashed, defaced. They demanded retribution, blood, his, and quarts of it, would be adequate. I calmed the group by assuring them I would deal with the offense appropriately, to the severest of the severity allowed by home policy and the law.

I put on my finest therapist's hat and I called Johnny

to the office for a heart to heart. I was compassionately Rogerian, I was directively Glasserian, analytically Freudian, Adlerian, Ellisian. I tried to help him understand the social consequences of his actions. I tried to get to the bottom of this rage and rottenness in him. I tried to get him to connect with his feelings, anything meaningful within him. I wanted to break through his steel resolve to shun healing human involvement. I fished with every bait I knew for his misery and pain. But he never took the bait. He was a shark and he went after me. Every word of compassion I uttered was matched by epithets and curses, suggestions and recommendations regarding my sexual conduct and relationships. Those I'd heard plenty; I'd gotten used to them. It was not his words that finally brought up the gorge of rage in me, but it was his absolute refusal to let me be competent, adequate, professional, spiritual, and yes, his savior. I finally gave up. In a stoically controlled monotone voice that was calculated to mask my rage, I banished him to his room to "think about what we had talked about." I would not give him the victory, the pleasure of knowing he had ME nailed down. He went and immediately began beating the walls and doors, screaming hatred and vengeance on me and the household. Again, the lynch mob assembled at the office door; they knew I had failed to control this volcano of misery.

James, a budding sociopath whom I feared would become (and truly, to this day I think is) a serial killer somewhere, and who was always the spokesman for the mob, looked at me accusingly, "Well, what are you gonna do, huh? If it was me I'd kick his butt."

"You would, huh?" I listened to the pounding, and I felt the pounding my ego had taken.

Yes. James.

"You would like that, wouldn't you, James?"

"Yeah, me and everyone else. Ain't that right, guys? But you guys won't let us fight him 'cause it's against the rules. And I ain't getting grounded 'cause of that jerk." James always looked out for himself.

"Well, James, you only get grounded if I catch you fighting. And if there aren't any witnesses, well. . . . "

"So what are you sayin'? We can kick John's butt and we won't get grounded?"

"Yeah, if that's what you guys really want to do, I guess so. You wait outside by the dumpster after dinner and I'll have him take out the garbage for his chore. You guys will have two minutes. Then I'll come out and you guys take off, and I didn't see anything. Got it?"

"Yeah! Alright! We're gonna kill him!"

And after dinner, a strangely quiet dinner in which everyone, especially James and I, were extremely polite and asked John, "More peas, John? Get you some more milk, John? Take your plate to the kitchen for you, John?"

HOW I AM

the deed was done.

I sent Johnny, a scowling, dirty, swaggering sixty pound human bag of hate and venom out the door with a sack of garbage. And I stood at the picture window and watched the ambush, the short dance of bravado that precedes an elementary schoolboy's fight, and the beating. Expressionless, I watched. He brought it on himself. He must understand there are consequences for antisocial behavior. He must understand that he cannot wantonly destroy other people's things. Especially their egos. My ego.

When I thought he'd had enough I opened the front door and turned on the porchlight. The mob scattered into the dusk leaving Johnny lying, curled up in a ball on the dirt like a flicked potato bug. He took his dusty arm from over his head to look up to see why his assassins fled and saw me strolling, too casually, to where he lay.

He uncurled and lifted himself from the ground, his sixty pound frame shaking uncontrollably. And when he stood up I saw a child. A small, scared, lonely, beaten child with furrows engraved by tears in the dirt on his face. A rejected child who raised a skinny arm, and sighting down his trembling finger pointed at me he cried through huge gasps of breath, "You! You're just like them! You don't care, you don't. See how you are? See? I thought you were different, but you're just like them!"

And he was right. I saw how I was. Clearly. Just like

"them." My piety, self-righteousness, knowledge, wisdom, selflessness, spirituality, competence and religion became my idols and I destroyed a child who threatened to tear them down. I was a deviser of plots. A maker of unholy alliances. A betrayer. A murderer by proxy.

I was just like "them," the crucifiers of the Christ.

Yes, and I am still like them. Expose my weaknesses, question my competence, doubt my integrity, prove me a fool, show my ignorance, discover my pretenses, unmask my hypocrisy, bring me down a notch or two, threaten my status, undermine my power, jeopardize my position, do any of these to me and I will save myself. I will preserve my ego, my proud images at any price. I will leave you, fire you, cast shadows of doubt on your competence and integrity, gossip about you or quit. I will call you a fool, unbelieving, hard-headed or ignorant. I will crucify you. Believe it, because I am just like them.

I am just like those who took The Child who would not allow us the pleasures of our proud delusions and hung him on a cross.

I see the quivering hand that was once held out in healing and compassion now nailed down by the sins of proud humanity and I understand what the cross says about all of us, yes even me, "See how you are, see how you really are?"

But he let us do it, for our sakes. For the sake of the self-righteous, the betrayers, the devisors of plots and makers of unholy alliances, the murderers by proxy, the crucifiers. I see his hands nailed down and his voice call out for our forgiveness and I understand what the cross says about God, "See how I am, see how I really am?"

CHAPTER SEVENTEEN
O HOME, CHILD

> *All these died in faith, without receiving the promises, but having seen them and having welcomed them from a distance, and having confessed that they are strangers and exiles on the earth. For those who say such things make it clear that they are seeking a country of their own.*
>
> Hebrews 11:13-14

In the days of Woodstock, peace signs and paisley Nehru jackets I could not reconcile the concepts of God's love, forgiveness, mercy, justice, punishment and wrath. I believed that it was cruel and inhuman to deliberately inflict pain and suffering on another human being as retribution for doing wrong. (Not that I now have them all reconciled precisely or adequately, but I live in peace knowing that this will not be a fifty point essay question on the final exam.) In those days when I believed "all you need is love" (actually I still do, but my definition of love has more to do with Jesus than John Lennon now), I served as a social worker and family therapist for a residential treatment agency for emotionally disturbed boys.

Skinny Jimmy was one of the first kids I worked with from intake to discharge. His case history read like some twisted fiction. There was the "usual" abuse and neglect: left home unsupervised, unfed, bruises from repeated beatings over spilled milk, slamming the front door and such things. Then there was his closet. He was tied up, beaten and put in it to sleep and eat for a week or more at a time for not making his bed properly. And the lit matches and cigarettes applied to his pale skin. Even those things, in the dirges of abuse and neglect, become a common refrain over the years. The first time you read such things you weep, the twenty-second time you shake your head. But then, in Skinny Jimmy's case, there were the parts where I could not even shake my head. It was (and still is) beyond my comprehension what a child's mind does with seeing his father in the back yard engaging in sexual intercourse with the family's dog. Or where a child puts into his fragile psychological framework, being made to eat his own feces as punishment for messing his pants. You have the words describing the abuse. You are probably shaking your head in disbelief. I had the flesh and blood of the victim in my care and custody. When a freckled face and skinny arms and knobby knees and cowlick give flesh to the words of a case history your stomach does somersaults.

My "peace, love and eternal cosmic harmony" outlook on the world was having difficulty standing up under such an onslaught of human depravity. My rigid pacifistic views were bent to splintering, and my sense of pity and understanding for those less fortunate (socially, psychologically, spiritually and emotionally) went up in smoke in my hot, vengeful indignation. I wanted to show up at our first family therapy session with a baseball bat and do my small part to even up the cosmic balance of pain and suffering inflicted on this innocent. Yes, yes, I jumped through all the psychological and biblical non-judgmentalism hoops; I rationalized every way I could. I tried to pity them: his parents were abused as children themselves. I distanced myself from them as "clients," I got close to them as lost souls, and I tried to separate the sin from the sinner. And I still wanted to see them suffer for their evil deeds. I wanted to hear them beg for mercy from someone bent on justice, incapable of feeling mercy, just like their children had probably cried out to them. I would have burned my ACLU card to help God kindle the fire of hell under THEIR feet to make them pay for the unthinkable things they inflicted on this child.

Spare me any letters either defending or reprimanding me for my reactions, thank you. I have alternately done both to myself, for far longer and probably with far greater earnestness and severity than you could possibly muster. So far I have come to this: There simply are no theoretical or theological frameworks that will contain the human gut reaction to the scars and bruises inflicted on the helpless, defenseless, trusting, and weak. Actually, this is all beside the point because I am not here to intellectually discuss the problem of pain, nor justify or condemn my, or your, emotional response to suffering.

Nor am I going to discuss God's response (or complain about his seeming non-response) to suffering, nor make the obvious point that Jesus died for even those horrors, that even those sins were nailed to his cross. Nor am I going to tell you how God watched as his own child was mercilessly abused and murdered, then incomprehensibly turned his face from him as he cried out for his Father's merciful presence. I do not have the understanding nor the words yet to tell that.

No, I wish to tell you about something simpler, but something more mysterious, than even the abuse and neglect of Jimmy. I would not have known it, nor have guessed it, but I have seen it. It is this: given the choice to stay in a secure, nurturing, positive, consistent, loving foster family or going home to more abuse and neglect, out of forty or so children we kept over five years, there were only two or three that did not want to go home.

Many of them did go home, only to be abused again and removed again. All of them lived with a tension between the desire to go home and the knowledge of what home held for them. They knew too well from what they had come and to what they would return. Though some held on to fantasies about things being better, by the time we dealt with the realities through home visits and therapy, most held few illusions about how things really were. And they still wanted to go home. It was not that they hated us, we just were not home.

"Unless you become like little children you cannot enter the kingdom," Jesus says. As adults we look at the Skinny Jimmies and our rational, reasonable, practical adult minds shift into high gear. We look at a relationship (any relationship) and we tally up the abuse, the hurt, the pain, the destruction and fear, we worry about the future, and somewhere along the line we say, "It's not worth it." In Jimmy's case we worried about when he would get his next meal, his next word of praise, his next hug, his next goodnight kiss, his next pat on the head, his next time of laughter, his next heart to heart. But Jimmy did not tabulate the pain and the insecurity and the destructiveness. He did not count the missed meals, the hours in the closet, the number of welts, the days without a kind word. He did not concern himself with worries about his next meal or hug or praise. All he knew was home. It was mom and dad. It was where he belonged. In the deepest part of his guts and in his heart of hearts he knew home was where he was supposed to be. Jimmy might have changed his mind when he grew up and learned to count sins and worry about tomorrow's food and hugs and words. Until he did, he wanted to be home at any cost.

Home is a relentless urge, an irresistible call that

transcends counting sorrows and pain, the sins against us, that runs deeper than biology, that cannot be changed by "adult" reasonings. We must dwell in the place to which our hearts call us.

Perhaps this is a small part of what Jesus meant by becoming like little children. It is responding to the relentless urge within us that is deeper than bookkeeping and biology: the call to the kingdom, the place we know is truly home. It transcends the need for predictability, the security of knowing where we will be living and how and when we will get our strokes and laughs. It is setting aside our worrisome adult thinking, our tabulations of assets and liabilities, the reasonableness and practicality of living in one place or the other, in one way or another. Hebrews chapter eleven tells us how all the great examples of faith, like children, lived with uncertainty, sorrows, trauma, pain, unpredictability, and sometimes terror simply because they opened their hearts to the call to home. The wanderings, the uncertainty, the homelessness, the terror, the unknown, the hunger and thirst, and even death – none of it mattered because they knew somewhere, somehow, in the deep of their hearts it all had to do with going home.

I've thought now and again about Jimmy and the parting look he gave us when he finally left us to go home. It was difficult to accept then. In one sense I felt we deserved better – at least a glimmer of sadness for having to leave us, a smile of gratitude for all we did, or a wistful backwards glance as he walked away.

(Those are considered some of the "rewards" of foster care.) But he, like many others, gave us none of those. Now I see the heart of the child, not my ledgerbook of good deeds we had done for him and the evil deeds his parents had done against him. Home is where the heart is, not necessarily where the stomach is fed, the sheets are clean, the TV works, and you get treated fairly and squarely. Home is where no one counts the good and evil, the blessings and curses. Home is where, just for today, it is good enough just to be there.

When I walk away from this world to go home, I only hope that I can look back at it like Jimmy and so many others looked back at us as they walked away: with contempt. Because, you see, I'll be leaving and going home.

CHAPTER EIGHTEEN
THE TEMPTATION OF FRANK

This story is true. It was a Bible class teacher's nightmare become reality.

If you have taught for any length of time you will understand this: It was one of those times when you feel the reply that came out of your mouth was given by inspiration from On High because you were still reeling from the blind side sucker punch comment from one of the class members.

THE LORD OF THE HUNT

It was a Sunday morning adult Bible class. We were discussing temptation, specifically, Jesus' ability to empathize with our temptations because he was tempted in all the same ways we are. I was confessing to the class that I used to have a hard time believing Jesus' temptations were really the same as mine. We read the temptation account from Matthew 4:1-11. I said that I didn't know about them, but personally, I was never tempted to turn stones to bread. Nor was I ever taken to the top of the Valley Bank Plaza downtown and tempted to hurl myself down to see if God would give me wings or something. And I was never, ever taken on a world tour by Satan and offered it all if I would just bow down and worship him.

A timid hand went halfway up. It was Frank.

Frank was labelled by the doctors as a functioning chronically mentally ill person. He could hold a job between his hospital stays and "mild episodes" as they were benignly called.

"Yes, Frank."

"That happened to me last week."

Fifty-something pairs of eyes went front, twenty some-odd people sat up in their seats. Class just got REALLY interesting.

The point of the class was that temptation is temptation. There are the generic classifications like the

THE TEMPTATION OF FRANK

flesh, the eyes, pride, then there are all the specifics that fall under the category headings. (Oh, yes. Frank. I'll tell you what happened later.)

Was Jesus tempted in all points like me? My feeling had always been "Probably not, really," though I HAD to say he was because the scriptures say he was. But as I got to know Jesus and as I was able to be more honest with myself about my own weaknesses, I was forced to continually re-evaluate that feeling. It started with obvious things, like Jesus owned a construction business and so do I.

Maybe Jesus never was tempted to pad his bill to a customer when he knew his family was short for rent that week. Maybe he was never tempted to hide a few items when the taxman came around to collect.

No, I suppose he wouldn't have been tempted to make up some excuse or find a "nice way" to put off a slow pay client, or avoid having to deal with an annoying person. And while I'm at it, I guess he was never tempted:

to take a "short-cut" (oh, the short-cuts he could have taken!) to get a project done because he couldn't finish in time or was losing money on it,

to casually drop a few "little known facts" about someone in a conversation just to let the people around him know that he was "in the know," to take advantage of someone's gullibility and trusting nature to get something for next to nothing,

to get arrogant because he was popular,

to use his resources to indulge himself, just a little bit, because he deserved it after all,

to avoid conflicts by disappearing, putting people on hold until they went away, or simply ignoring them,

to yell at someone because he was bone tired, had a headache and had just beat his thumb with a hammer or been interrupted for the fourth time,

to seduce (or allow himself to be seduced by) any one of the women who adored him, especially when he was feeling depressed, misunderstood, and rejected,

to chuckle or laugh condescendingly at someone's ignorance, failure or stupidity,

to pretend he didn't see that woman in tears, that man sitting alone, staring at his own hands in a knot in his lap,

to look at someone suffering and tell himself he didn't need to help them because it was their own fault, they deserved it, that they made their bed, now they can sleep in it,

THE TEMPTATION OF FRANK

to seek pity, to ask for breaks, or to get attention by playing up how hard his life was,

to take one more cup of wine, the one that would soften the hard edges of the world for a while,

to take the drug that would kill the pain in his body and the unfathomable loneliness of his soul when he was forsaken by all creation and the Creator.

Or maybe he was, in all this and more. (I am sure the list could go on like War and Peace.) And maybe because of his God-ness he knew temptation like I could never know it. His burdens were infinitely weightier than mine, his knowledge infinitely greater, his love infinitely more passionate, and his sorrows infinitely deeper. Consequently his temptations to abuse, misuse, escape, mistreat, look down on, bail out, check out, and short-cut were infinitely greater. Yet he was without sin.

I think the reason I've never been tempted to turn stones to bread is because I have already fallen to the far lesser temptation to turn a padded timecard into bread, or a stereo, or a new tire, or a payment on Mastercharge.

I don't think I've ever been tempted to trade a moment's worship of Satan for the whole world because I've traded a moment with him for far less. The extra hour on the paycheck, the bask in the limelight, the moment of freedom, the praise of people I couldn't really care less about, the raise, even the two dollar item the cashier forgot to ring up. I don't need the whole world, or Manhattan, or even Yuma, I'll fall down for loose change and a ten second rush of gratification, amusement, gloating, comfort, or acceptance.

Which, I guess, brings me back to Frank, who was offered the whole world. I suppose you'd like to know how it turned out?

I said, "Thank you for sharing that with us, Frank. Obviously you did not fall for the temptation since you are here with us tonight. That's great."

Frank smiled.

The members smiled.

The class went on.

CHAPTER NINETEEN
HIS FAITHFULNESS IS EVERLASTING

William's world was one he gave few people the privilege of entering. Then again, few people had any interest in seeing the stuff his private, inner "great wall" was made of. He was the fifth generation of crazies. Our staff psychiatrist told us when a mother and son have an incestuous relationship for years it always results in some sort of insanity. William's was of many sorts. His was a Whitman's Sampler of craziness, one could only guess what was at the center of his different behaviors, one could only be certain there were nuts.

The first time I visited William's mother to assess her for home visits for him I nearly vomited. Indelicate of me to say so, yes, but sadly true. I made my way down the glass strewn alley, between the cars on blocks and around the overflowing bashed and tilted garbage cans to her apartment door. I knocked. Waited. Knocked. The door knob turned as slowly as in a murder mystery and the door meandered open about six inches. I stepped forward as a face and body appeared to fill the void, "Mrs. Howard?" A plague of flies as if shot from a scattergun blew out the opening, and a smell, no, a stench, threw me backwards, gagging. It was William's mother, and her odor, at the door.

The evaluation was one of my first as a social worker. Objectivity and professionalism were hard to come by as I watched fifty or more cockroaches crawl the walls behind the olive green naugahyde chair, patched wantonly with peeling silver duct tape, that she dumped her great rolls of flesh in. I never turned around to see what was crawling behind me. Nonjudgmentalism was nearly impossible when her face went blank as a paper plate in mid-sentence and she began to talk to God about me. And he answered her. At least so she said. I told her since God said it was OK to listen to me, I wanted her to take a bath and clean her house before our next visit. She did, and for every visit thereafter for the next few years of our acquaintance. I don't think she kept bathing after William was placed back home with her.

William made a little more sense to me after that visit. But not much. Just enough to remind me not to expect miracles, or more precisely, to redefine what is a miracle in his case. It was a miracle to get him to tie his shoes, after the miracle of getting him to wear them. It was miracle when he stopped stealing food and hoarding it in his room, fudgsicles under his pillow, a can of corn in his shoes (without the can), leftover pancakes stashed under his mattress. The grandest miracle was when he stopped running away.

William came to us from the state mental hospital. When he came to live with us we had been at the home for about a month. He was eleven going on two. His case history was filled with psychological mumbo jumbo I didn't understand at the time and I didn't have the humility to ask what it all meant. Some things I did understand. One was that he was a runner. When he got frustrated or anxious he'd run away from home, foster homes, the state hospital.

He ran away the first hour he was with us. He was anxious. A new house, new rules, new routines, new counselors, seven new roommates. We had to chase him and drag him back, literally. No help from him at all, two furrows in the dirt from the backs of his heels, a hundred yards' worth from the road to the driveway. He ran three times that day. We dragged him back three times. We told him each time, "This is your home now. If you run, we will find you and bring you back here. Always. We promise." We wore out the heels of his shoes over the next month. We dragged him home twice a day for a week. Then once a day for a couple weeks. Then once every two or three days.

Successive approximations our psychologist called it. Small changes and occasional setbacks that ultimately get closer to the goal. William eventually would walk back with us instead of having to be dragged back. After a couple months we didn't even chase him, he would come back after five or six hours, and always before dinner. Six months, he would run to the edge of the property and stand by the tree, looking at the house. Eight months, he would go out the back door and sit in the corner of the back porch for ten minutes. A year, he would just go to his room.

His last four years with us were spent in successive approximations of every conceivable human activity. Personal hygiene, dressing, waking up, going to bed, eating. And social skills, talking, playing, group activities, conversation skills, public behavior, manners. All successive approximations, every change a birthing, laborious, agonizing and glorious to behold.

When William was no longer deemed crazy he was allowed to go home to his mother. Back to the incest. Back to her voices and being isolated from the world, back to the hours and hours of TV, back to ditching school. He eventually dropped out to watch TV with his mother. When we left the home we lost touch with him.

Four years later, late one winter's night, William,

then twenty, called me. He said, "I just wanted to tell you thanks. I know it's been a long time but I got kind of screwed up when I went back home, you know. But last year I was sitting there watching TV with my mom and all of a sudden it was like everything you guys ever told me made sense, like about being responsible for my behavior and not looking for excuses. So I told my mom if I stayed with her I would never amount to anything and I moved out and got a job at McDonald's. I got my GED and I'm in a school learning carpentry. I know you guys tried real hard and I was kind of a jerk when I was with you but I wanted to let you know I'm gonna make it. Thanks for everything. I love you guys."

That was the last I've heard from William. I know he'll "make it" because whether he knew it or not, he made it the first day he came to live with us. We chose him and would not let him go. He ran and we sought him. And the work of our seeking was manifested in his becoming what we hoped for by successive approximations, and finally in the miracle of a phone call late one winter's night.

The life of faith is much like William's successive approximations. Jacob's relationship with God was one based on God's promise that he would be with Jacob no matter what, and Jacob still spent most of his life running away from his problems and wrestling with God. Nicodemus began seeking Jesus in the dead of night and finally took him into his arms publicly from the cross. Thomas began by being chosen and in the end declared only a willingness to believe unless Jesus showed up, in the flesh, scars and all. Each manifested the work of the promise of God in small but miraculous ways and yet all were living by faith.

We tend to define faith by the end result, the grandest miracle of the phone call home. But faith is at the beginning, from the first day when God leaves the ninety-nine and drags you home by your heels just like he promised he would, and the next day or week or lifetime you run from him one less time. God knows where we've come from and knows that our changes are often successive approximations. The important thing is not how quickly, slowly, completely or partially we change but that we are in his house struggling toward the miracles.

Yes, some day it will all become clear, it will finally make sense and we will be changed by God's own last and best miracle into what we've tried to be all along. But understand until then that for now faith is simply knowing you are already home just because God has promised you are.

1980'S
PART FOUR

J ...AND ESUS WAS A CARPENTER

CHAPTER TWENTY

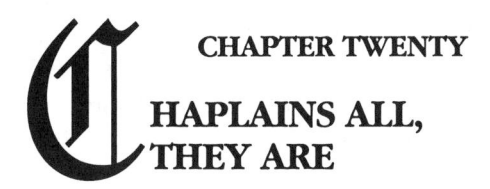

CHAPLAINS ALL, THEY ARE

> *Then Satan answered the Lord, "Does Job fear God for nothing? Hast Thou not made a hedge about him and his house and all that he has, on every side? Thou hast blessed the work of his hands, and his possessions have increased in the land. But put forth Thy hand now and touch all that he has; he will surely curse Thee to Thy face.*
> *Job 1:9-11*

This not to boast. In fact, by the time I am done with what I am about to say you will understand how ashamed I am to admit it.

I had compassion on the homeless and street people long before they became fashionable objects of concern. I was accused more than once of preaching a "social gospel." I railed at and about the suited, cologned congregations I attended. I spoke passionately at Bible studies, in Sunday school classes, and with my friends about them. But I preached from a comfortable distance from the homeless and the hungry. True, I handed out spare change to vagrants a few times when I happened to be downtown. Over the years my wife and I took in a few questionable characters until we had our children and found out once we had housed a child molester.

It was January in Phoenix. As usual, the city was swollen with jobless, homeless people who migrate here because of the mild winter. I, too, was job hunting. My elders and I had come to a mutual agreement that I was not "effective" as an associate minister. They graciously gave me six months to find another job. Before I ended up starting my construction company I looked at nearly everything under the sun. I almost took jobs as a juvenile probation officer, a treatment program manager for a prison, a representative for a blood bank, or a director of a foster care program for the aged. The help wanted ad that really caught my eye was for a chaplain for a downtown shelter for the homeless. A soup kitchen, tent city and social service center with a spiritual commitment. I was ecstatic. My degrees in theology, counseling, and my social work experience, all of my personal commitments focused at last. I called and set up an interview.

The day of the interview I put on my interviewing suit, a dark blue pinstripe job, and my red "power tie." I drove downtown. Deep downtown. As I neared the address of the shelter the cityscape began looking more and more tired and beaten down. The people began looking more and more weary, more hardened, more threatened and threatening. To my left I saw a line of people leaning against the face of a building, a human bar graph of pain, some standing, some squatted down, some lying down, some hunched over. As I drove by them looking for the address I discreetly punched the lock on my door with my elbow. I found the building and realized they were the line for the shelter. Over a hundred people standing in line at two o'clock for a few beds and a meal offered first-come first-served when the doors opened at five. I drove back around the building looking for a parking place. From this direction I was looking into their faces. Some stared back at me.

I never made the interview. I never even parked my car. I just drove on. I did not unlock my doors until I got home.

I was afraid of them. I looked upon them with their matted, greasy hair and their mismatched thrift store clothing. I looked upon the robotic drunks with their empty stares. I saw the fearful hugging themselves, embracing blankets and bags of rags to their empty stomachs. I saw their shopping carts with bags of cans guarded like they were armored cars full of gold. I saw the Jonahs running from God, the Jacobs running from their own doings, the Jobs suffering without cause, the Onesimuses escaping responsibility, the Prodigal sons, the Gerasene demoniacs covered with self-inflicted wounds. Most disturbing were the children so young yet unintimidated by the fearfulness around them. I saw sheep without a shepherd, lost, hungry, dying, helpless, wounded and tired. I saw the psychos, like wolves preying on the weak, the fearful, and the alone. I saw the timid crazies trying to blend seamlessly into the wall to avoid being picked on. I saw them and I was afraid.

I feared, I think, what they would do to me. Not physically, but emotionally and spiritually. I would be a chaplain, a man of God, a priest, a comforter, a teacher of God's will and purposes. You ask what could they possibly do to me that would fill me with such terror that I would walk away from them? I will tell you: I was afraid they would ask me, "Why?"

"Why am I suffering?"

"Why am I hungry?"

"Why am I lonely?"

"Why can't I find work?"

"Why can't I get the help I need to get back on my feet?"

"Why did God do this to me?"

"Why has God done this to all these other people?"

"Why are these children suffering?"

"Why have I been forsaken?"

CHAPLAINS ALL, THEY ARE

"Why are you sitting there in a suit with a full belly telling me to trust God?"

"Why do you believe there is a God in the face of all this?"

I was afraid of them because they had the right to ask me why and I would have no answers. They would ask me why I had no answers. They would ask me if there is an answer. I suddenly felt like all my college degrees had imparted not wisdom but platitudes. Words with the substance and weight of fog. They would ask me how it is I can serve God without answers, perhaps I serve only because I am comfortable, I have a house, a car, a job, my children go to bed with a full belly every night. I was afraid all I could say is, "Where were you when God created the world?" (Job 38:4). I was afraid because that answer never seemed good enough to me either. I was afraid they would ask me to pray and they would return prayed for but still hopeless, crazy, jobless and hungry. I was afraid they would ask God's will and I could not tell it. I was afraid they would seek God and he would be silent.

I was afraid I would be found out for what I am: a man of God. A man. Just a man. Fed and clothed and in my right mind by all earthly standards, but just as desperate for answers and as much in the dark about God and his ways as the least of these.

So I went home and wept.

I did not weep for them. It was for myself. Their Job-like lives ripped my formulations of faith and God from the intellectual realms of theory, doctrine and church dogma. Faith was suddenly no longer whose church dogma is correct but who can believe while sitting on the ash heap, covered with boils and not knowing why. My theology was first and foremost propositional, believe correctly and you will live. Their theology was interrogatory, can I believe there is a God who is love? It was not that I had never asked the questions, but I was never so violently and painfully forced to confront them. Perhaps Satan could rightfully accuse me of serving God gratuitously, because I am blessed (Job 1:9-10). Perhaps given the ash heap and boils I would curse God and die.

Perhaps in my pride I had railed at the wrong people. I fancied myself a prophet like Jeremiah, calling for justice, mercy and compassion from a stiff-necked people. I suddenly realized that role was too easy on me to be real, my words were just self-righteous rhetoric, an intellectualized theological arrogant social worker's tongue-lashing. It came from my inflated spiritual ego. There was a piece missing that I only recently came to understand.

I had railed against God's people. The homeless made me realize that it was God I needed to rail at. Let me explain.

I had questioned God once in a while – we all do – but I had never railed at God. But I realize now the reason I never railed at him was not because of my great faith and love for him. It was because I never truly allowed God to touch me wholly, to enter the very darkest and deep places of my very world and existence. I held him superficially, conveniently. All the great men of God railed at God, wrestled with God, questioned God, challenged God, and bargained with God. They cursed their anointings, they resisted their calls. Moses, Abraham, Jacob, David, Job, Jeremiah, Jonah. God moved in on them, he grasped them with a love that would not let them go and they cursed and squirmed. And it was counted as faith: they were friends of God, men after God's own heart, prophets, lovers of God, loved by God. It was through this they could say with Job, "I have heard about you with the hearing of the ear; but now my eye sees you" (Job 42:5). He was the God of experience, not theory.

I had never believed in him through a veil of tears. I had never heard him above the sound of my own shrieking in pain or terror. I had never sat in the dark and found light in him only. He was the God I had heard about but not seen, that I could talk about but not feel passion for. I had belief, perhaps, but little faith. I had but little love, the kind of love that only comes from knowing a God who is here, right here in all this, my own terror, hunger, craziness, sin, darkness and weakness, not out there silently watching his creation slowly die in torment.

Over the years I have let God in. When I have I've railed against him, begged, bargained, pleaded, and resisted him. But I've come to know the love that will not let me go even though I still do not know where I was when he created the world.

I thank God for that line of shabby, stricken, lazy, crazy, sad and hopeless street people in need of a chaplain. They were the ones covered with boils, sitting on the ash heap to whom I went, like Job's friends, to minister to with a God of religion. Instead they were a hundred something chaplains to me. In the end it was they, like Job was for his friends, who were qualified to pray for me and restore me to God (Job 42:8).

I tell you, be careful. The next person you meet that you think needs your help because he is resisting God, questioning God's integrity and justice, and railing against the judgments of God may be the very person you need to restore you to God. He may be Job or Jacob or Jeremiah. His ash heap life may in the end have more profound influence on the whole world than all the religion in the world put together.

CHAPTER TWENTY-ONE
RALPH

I saw Ralph in the front seat of one of my employees' cars. He was on the way to the pound. The look on his face said, "Take me home," so I did.

Ralph was a large dog. At five months old he could stand with his paws on my shoulders and look me in the face. It soon became obvious Ralph was going to be difficult to live with.

Ralph had no sense of what were his toys and our

precious belongings. He dragged tables and chairs into the yard. My weight bench. The wheel barrow. Two by fours. Laundry. He didn't even seem to catch on that gardenias are for smelling, not lying on, and planters are for gazing at, not running gleefully through. His joyful leaping when someone came out of the house was like being charged by a crazed elephant. And as with most dogs, he barked when he thought we were being threatened, mostly when we didn't want to hear it, at 2:00 a.m. He was unmanageable, impossible to contain.

So we gave him away. Not that we really wanted to, but we had to, kind of.

I say "kind of" because when I thought about it I found more at work here than just a dog playing with my lawn furniture. It is like the world "kind of had to" crucify Christ.

Yes, it is a stretch, but hear me out.

Jesus came and began playing with all the precious things people owned. The ritual tools they worked with for God, their comfortable doctrinal furniture they sat in to be in his presence, the traditional tables on which they spread their religious goodies out before God. He played with things too big for him, things about God that he dragged into the streets from the pious confines of the temple.

Like Ralph, he never quite seemed to enjoy things

according to the rules. Wine was for drinking and food was for eating. Ordinary people were for talking to and being friends with. Sinners were for forgiving. Sick people were for healing. Poor people were for giving to and feeding. Dead people were for raising.

And he warned people whenever he thought they were being threatened by some unseen menace. Regardless of the time or place, whether people wanted to hear it or not, he spoke out. He was impossible to manage, he was too wild to contain.

So they had to get rid of him, kind of.

Look in your own religious back yard, your private places, neatly fenced off from everyone else's view. What has Jesus done there? Perhaps he has demolished your carefully cultivated notions of God. Maybe his grace has upset your table of neatly arranged doctrines and dug holes under your fences, your boundaries of fellowship. He may even be trying to warn you about something terribly wrong invading your life.

If your yard is neat and tidy, maybe he hasn't been there.

If it is a mess, there's a good chance he's been there.

So, now what are you going to do with him?

CHAPTER TWENTY-TWO

THE GOSPEL ACCORDING TO STEAMED ZUCCHINI

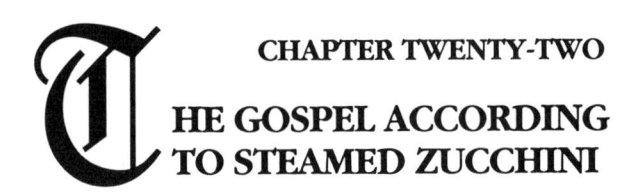

> *Jesus therefore said to them, "Truly, truly, I say to you, unless you eat the flesh of the Son of Man and drink His blood, you have no life in yourselves."*
>
> John 6:53

I am sitting in a wire-framed, molded plastic chair in the cafeteria of St. Joseph's Hospital. My crew just finished morning break and went back to the seventh floor where we are remodeling the patient wing. The nurses and orderlies are returning to their duties, a doctor or two straggles in and out for a donut and coffee.

I watch the procession of doctors and nurses, surgeons with long slender piano-virtuoso fingers, clip-boards, surgical gowns and stethescopes. I watch the lines of staff, patients and loved ones at the food counters and I wonder from where they've come.

From the flash of scalpels.

From the punctuated breathing of the hopelessly injured.

From the beeps and clicks of machine-sustained life.

From the smell of clinical cleanliness.

From the shedding of blood.

From the silent raging.

From the unspoken hopes.

From the quiet resignations.

From the fulfillment and end of dreams.

The inexorable circle of life is being completed by some, it is beginning for some. Others are here to prolong the closing of the circle. Others are here to observe the closing of the circle. Life and death. They all come to the cafeteria having confronted the mystery of life and death, whether from the operating rooms, the patient rooms, the research labs, or the autopsy lab.

THE GOSPEL ACCORDING TO STEAMED ZUCCHINI

From the glint of scalpels to the flash of butterknives.

From the sharp prick of needles to the stab of a fork.

From the bottles of manufactured life-fluids to paper cups full of liquid concoctions.

From bloodshed and the lifesaving mutilation of bodies to meat loaf and hot dogs.

Few suspect it, but it is not in the operating rooms, or the laboratories, or the patient rooms that the mysteries of life and death are revealed. It is there that the questions arise. It is here, in the cafeteria that the answer is found. There before them, on melmac plates, in paper cups, in styrofoam bowls, on plastic trays lies the answer to the mystery, the questions of life and death that few have the words or even the courage to ask.

The answer is simply this: It is not that death is the end of life, but that life comes from death. From the sacrifice of some animal or vegetable's life, now steamed, sauteed, deep fried or broiled, another life is sustained. But the mystery is deeper still; the thing that died becomes a part of the living and in a mystery is alive again, transformed, raised up a new life within the one for whom it died. Death and life. It is not the saving of a life or the perpetuation of life in its known and present form that is the grandest miracle, but the transformation of life through death.

. . . Christ died for our sins according to the Scriptures . . . (I Corinthians 15:3).

If we have died with Christ we believe we shall also live with him (Romans 6:8).

One died for all therefore all have died. And he died for all, that those who live might no longer live to themselves but for him who for their sake died and was raised (II Corinthians 5:14-15).

If any man is in Christ he is a new creature, behold the old things have passed away and all things have become new (II Corinthians 5:17).

Life and death. Life from death. The high mystery of grace on a cafeteria tray.

CHAPTER TWENTY-THREE
WHY, JAKE?

Jake was the foreman on a small office remodel we were doing. I worked with him for about four days. He was in his mid-fifties maybe, his manner a little crusty but still soft in some of the important places. He was good at shooting the bull, a skill most construction foremen develop to keep the owners ignorant and happy and the workers working with him instead of against him.

Jake had a tired air about him. It wasn't just the long

hours. You could catch him in the corridor when he wasn't aware you were there, when he thought he was "off camera" and you could see he was a weary man.

We had to work a long weekend to finish the job on schedule. Jake had to open and close the offices for us so I asked him when it was convenient for him to open and close. He said, "Anytime, I live alone now (the word "now" dangled conspicuously there in space), and I'm up a lot just watching TV anyway so call whenever and I'll come." I began listening to Jake. His conversations were salted, but not often, with veiled references to his empty house, his aloneness, his weariness. I never really found out what happened to his wife, all I gathered was that she was gone. I never quite figured out if it was by her choice, his or somehow else.

About six months later I heard from another foreman that Jake had committed suicide. Jake was the foreman on a church building in another city when he did it. The irony of it was bitter. A man so hopeless and helpless building a monument to the Only Hope there is and The Help of the helpless, who came in contact daily with ministers of healing, who finally cried "Enough!" and went away.

Why, Jake? Why did you feel you had to do it?

Jake, did you ever think to risk being human and ask someone for help? Or was it too much for your

WHY, JAKE?

macho construction foreman image to admit your hollow life and tears during midnight re-runs of "I Love Lucy"? Maybe you were, in your unwillingness to open up to someone about your most private sorrows, more human than any of us can admit to being. Maybe you were fully human, just as we are, in your glad handshake, your back-slaps and crude jokes that hid your trembling hands and your back bent over with burdens no one imagined.

Or was it, Jake, that you did risk looking human the only way you knew how, but no one noticed? Were the vague references to your empty house and your eternal TV vigil cries of desperation that no one heard? Jake, were we so caught up in a "godly" edifice that we were as cold and unfeeling as the stone and steel of our building? Jake, were you ever told by the building committee or pastor why the building was being built? Did they tell you it was because they needed more classroom space, an updated auditorium, a multi-purpose room, a better sound system? Did anyone tell you about the God that people come to that building to hear about? What did they tell you about him, Jake? Did they say "Oh, Jake, see how our God has blessed us with the material resources to build this building. He has prospered our congregation. God is so good to us." Did they ever mention how he binds up the brokenhearted and heals the wounded soul? Did anyone ever say, "Jake, I've been listening to you for a couple weeks. You seem lonely. Come over for dinner. Let's talk." Would you have turned them down, Jake? Would it have made any difference?

Jake, if you could hear me now, if it would make any difference to you, I would open my mouth and tell you that the only true answer to your pain and my questions is in Jesus Christ. The only hope we both have is in the gospel, the love of God for sinners so lost and unaware of what is going on around us and even within us.

Father, please have mercy on Jake, if indeed he needs it. Perhaps he was only reaching out in desperation for the hem of your garment, seeking a healing of something so deep inside that just kept bleeding no matter who on earth tried to heal it. I pray that you will heal him like you did another desperate bleeding soul who reached out for your hem so many years ago.

Have mercy on us, Father, we do indeed need it. Forgive us our trespasses against Jake. Forgive us our trespasses against the nameless souls who will pass through our lives untouched and unchanged because of our blindness and deafness to their veiled declarations of their broken hearts.

O, Father, heal us. Open our blind eyes, unstop our deaf ears, loosen our speechless tongues. Make us vessels of grace and peace. Give us the courage to heal. In the name of the one who sees, and hears, and was bruised for our healing. Amen.

CHAPTER TWENTY-FOUR

EARTHMAMA AND BILLY

And it happened that as He was reclining at the table in the house, behold many tax-gatherers and sinners came and joined Jesus and His disciples. And when the Pharisees saw this, they said to His disciples, "Why does your Teacher eat with the tax-gatherers and sinners?" But when He heard this, He said, "It is not those who are healthy that need a physician, but those who are ill. But go and learn what this means, 'I desire compassion and not sacrifice'; for I did not come to call the righteous, but sinners."
Matthew 9:10-13

You know the old joke. If you looked up the word "hippies" in the dictionary their picture would be there.

They were hired off the street as laborers by the general contractor. The labor pool consisted of the normal menagerie of just out of high school heavy metal types, drop-outs, punks, and jocks. Earthmama and Billy were twice the age of most of their fellow laborers and the years did not seem to have taken as much toll on them as the mileage. They were truly anachronisms beside the contemporary versions of societal rebellion.

Sparky (every electrician foreman is known as Sparky) was a good ol' boy in his fifties. Rednecks, I used to call them, but I've mellowed out some. He didn't have much good to say about Earthmama and Billy. "They oughta throw them in the pool, prob'ly ain't had a bath since 1968." "Someone oughta buy her a razor, teach her how to shave." Add sundry vulgar suggestions to the above and you have a measure of Sparky's regard for them. I never really understood why he would tell me these things because I have a beard and wear a pony-tail halfway down my back, much like Billy's. Well, Billy did have a glassy look in his eyes and a perpetual odor I didn't have. But for whatever reason, I was privy to Sparky's opinions of most everyone on the job, especially these two.

One day Billy came to work without Earthmama. He was particularly glassy-eyed. Strung out on drugs, Sparky suggested. Maybe tears, I thought. I asked Billy where Earthmama was, and he said she had passed out the day before on the way home (home, I found out, was a flop-house motel in the seediest part of downtown). He said he took her to a hospital but could not remember where it was. Being new in town and panic stricken he had just driven until he found one. I offered to help him find her if he could tell me her name. He didn't know her last name. They had lived together for about a month and he never knew her

EARTHMAMA AND BILLY

last name.

So I went to the job trailer and started calling all the hospitals in the vicinity of their motel. I had a first name, a description of her and the person who dropped her off. No Earthmama. Sparky wandered into the trailer with curious frequency. Between calls he looked at me, shook his head from side to side and said, "What the - - - - do you care about them for, they're nothing but a couple of worthless, filthy, - - - - - hippies."

I said, "Sparky, Billy is hurting because his old lady is in the hospital. If your wife was in the hospital you would be, too. And if it were you, I would do this same thing for you."

Sparky said, "- - - - ," and went out. He had a way with expletives.

Having no luck with the hospitals, I called my wife and sent her to their motel room to see if she had somehow gotten home. She was there. (Now, this is the very, very condensed version of a ten-hour story involving Billy's father, two hospitals in San Diego, an uneasy feeling on my way home from work, a recovering drug addict riding with me who learned compassion, the police, a stolen distributor cap and ripped out ignition wiring, a mechanic from our church who gave me a crash course on rewiring ignition systems on the phone, quartz crystals, karma, California and Christ. Perhaps I'll tell the whole thing in another book, but any more would be extraneous detail for my purposes here.) Back to that purpose.

The following day, mid-morning, Sparky caught me behind one of the buildings and said, "I thought about what you said yesterday. You know, you're right. What else is there in life if you don't care about people? How is she?"

I just told him, "She's O.K., thanks for asking."

I thought, "But Sparky, her healing is nothing compared to the healing that has taken place in you this day."

Ambassadors of grace, we are.

CHAPTER TWENTY-FIVE
ROLLING EYES

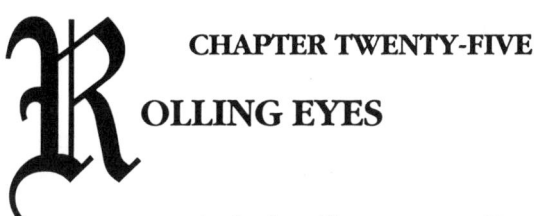

And when He came out, He saw a great multitude, and felt compassion for them, and healed their sick.
Matthew 14:14

I didn't know if the large greasy spot left on the block wall was from him or if it was the cumulative oil from the unwashed, sweaty backs of hundreds like him that hung as if by some invisible hook by the door of the convenience market looking for customers that might be easy touches. John and I must have looked easy, or it was because I broke the cardinal rule of avoiding panhandlers and made eye contact with him – it only takes one ten thousandth of a second. We got hit up for spare change. I don't remember which line he used but while he was going through his spiel, I looked over at John who looked at me. His eyes darted in the direction of the panhandler and then twisted skyward and slowly rolled down and around his sockets like a lazy roller coaster. You know the look.

In my business we ride a lot of elevators in the high-rise buildings downtown. An elevator ride is much like watching old comedy shows. Ernie Kovaks, Laugh-In, (for you younger readers, Hee-Haw). Short, fast vignettes, black-outs they used to be called. In an elevator you see someone for twenty, forty seconds and you get to guess their punch lines. We are dirty construction people in the midst of high finance, computers, new money, suits, pretense, paper fortunes and paper paupers. Their eyes roll at us, for certain. But we roll ours at them, too. The fifty something woman dressed in a revealing gauze blouse. The almost twenty woman in makeup that would clog the pores of Bozo the Clown. The fast track MBA in the latest haircut and IBM uniform speaking Wall Street-ese. The tired old guy in the year-before-last's lapels and tie with an unironed shirt. Hardly ever a word spoken, yet when the doors close behind them (and I am sure, behind us) what the eyes must do, what judgments are passed.

But what if, instead of rolling our eyes at people, we looked at them. What if, instead of a darting look in their direction we "fixed our gaze on them" (Acts 3:4), what would we see? I will tell you what you would see if you would see my crew. People covered with dirt, and covered with the same scars and bruises life has dished out to you. Single parents trying to raise kids, work and have a life of their own. Alcoholics, divorcees, people with education who cannot find jobs in their field, single people who can't find dates within the human species, husbands and fathers trying to pay bills, dying marriages, Little League coaches, people with kids in trouble, bank accounts overdrawn, spouses that just stare, some that scream, kid's birthday parties, lonely people, hurting people, happy people, phony people. People.

I look at people in the elevators (and everywhere, for that matter) and try to see their present facade as the cumulative effect of their history. The panhandler, is he lazy, crazy or sad? Is he the first or fifth generation of drunkards? Does he have, did he have, has he ever had a family, a father, a mother that he knows cares about him? The fifty-something woman whose looks have faded, has she ever known what it is to be loved for something precious inside her? Perhaps she has come to believe there is nothing inside her that is lovable. The old man in wrinkled clothes, is he a recent widower, a late in life divorcee? Is he tired because he is trying to keep from being pushed out by the mousse-haired kid behind him quoting Dow Jones industrials from memory? Was the made-up young woman abused as a child? Does she go home at night and weep at some ugliness she cannot hide with Mary Kay and Estee Lauder? Do the fashionable flirts go home to dark apartments and the flicker of video tapes in a dark bedroom, or to someone else's apartment and a flicker of passion they hope will light up their life with a true love? If we could only truly see.

So often the gospels say Jesus looked up, looked around, looked at, lifted his eyes and saw, he beheld. And every time he looked, he was moved. He felt compassion, he loved, he got angry, he had pity, he sighed. And each time he lifted his eyes to see, he felt, then he acted. Jesus never gave a sideways glance, never looked past someone, never gave his disciples a smirking "knowing look" behind someone's back.

Jesus never rolled his eyes. Because he looked, and he saw.

Perhaps what we do with our eyes is a mark of our spirituality. The nest time you catch yourself rolling your eyes, stop. Close your eyes, then open them. Fix your gaze on the human being before you and see, and wonder. Feel what goes on in the pit of your stomach. Then, like the apostles who said, "Silver and gold we don't have, but what we do have we give you, in the name of Jesus Christ . . .", do something. Give what you have, even if it is for a ten-second elevator ride, a smile, a sincere "Hello," a look of grace, an offering of peace. In the name of Jesus Christ.

CHAPTER TWENTY-SIX
ONE NIGHT ON THE PHONE

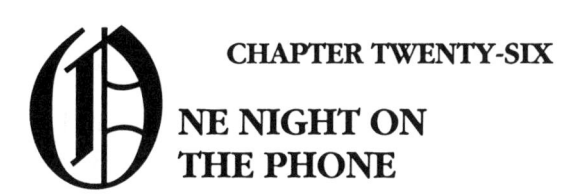

It is a Monday night.

I jotted some notes today at work, ideas for a new chapter or two. I'm sitting here to give them some flesh, some substance. The train of my thinking must not be derailed now, I am seeking that elusive phrase that will turn the ordinary thought into an inspiring spiritual insight for you.

And I'm getting frustrated, unhinged.

My phone just rang for the eighteenth time since 6:30 tonight. It is only 8:30. I know it will demand attention another fifteen times, at least, between now and 10:30. Listen. This is true stuff.

"I was supposed to meet Bill at the job, but he never showed up, so it didn't get done. Sorry I didn't call."

"Steve, this is Bill. The reason I didn't show up was I got arrested on the way in this morning and I just got out of jail. I can be there tomorrow but my tools are in my car and it's impounded."

"Hey, boss. I know I just got paid Friday but can I come over and get a week's advance tonight, my rent is due tomorrow."

"I need some help. Can you spare a couple of your people to help me out for a day or two?"

"Sorry I didn't show up today, but I forgot to set my alarm last night and woke up at noon, so I just blew it off. Hope I didn't put you in a bind."

"Did you see the letter the elders sent to all the Bible class teachers? I'm getting really fed up with that attitude in this church. I've got a good mind to leave."

"What am I going to do? John forgot to pick me up today and I got fired. It wasn't my fault."

ONE NIGHT ON THE PHONE

"I have a side-job that I really need to do tomorrow, can I have the day off?"

"What am I going to do with my son? I talk and talk and talk to him but he doesn't listen. Will you talk to him for me? Maybe he'll listen to a man."

"Could you keep Greg on another week? He owes me two hundred dollars, and if you fire him now, I'll never get it."

"I've got a brother-in-law who moved here last month and he's too lazy to look for a job. He's staying with us and I need him out of the house soon. Do you have any openings?"

"I know this is short notice, but can you have someone on my job at six tomorrow morning?"

"Sorry I didn't make it today, I forgot I had to take my mother to the Social Security office today. I'll need Thursday off, too."

"Can you do the youth group devotionals for the month of February?"

"A couple of your guys worked for me last week and I need to get their checks to them. Would you come to my office and pick them up and deliver them for me?"

"You'll have to find three more framers to cover the

hospital job. We got held up today at the office park and have to finish it tomorrow."

"I think George fell off the wagon last night. He never came home and, as far as I know, he never made it to work today for you either. You might be hearing from the job superintendent."

"What happened today? George said he'd have my job completed. I was there until three and he never showed."

All this (and more) while I'm trying to say something deep and spiritual about Jesus.

I literally cannot type one full sentence before the phone rings. Even while I am typing the transcript from the previous call . . . (There it went again.) I started three chapters tonight. Two sentences each. Great ideas, but I cannot collect a nickel's worth of thought before the phone rings yet again. So I've been writing my calls.

With each call I get more abrupt and terse.

"Yes. No. Fine. I'll let you know. Bye."

"Don't sweat it, someone will be there. Goodbye."

"Great. Just get some tools and show up tomorrow at six. And call if you can't make it this time."

ONE NIGHT ON THE PHONE

"I'm busy right now, I'll call you back when I can look at my calendar."

Now, where was I? Oh, yes . . . Jesus. I'm trying to write about Jesus.

Jesus,

who never ran a business,

who never had demanding clients,

who never had to meet deadlines,

who never had incompetent help,

who never got interrupted while he was engaged in important spiritual matters,

who never got tired of being dogged to death by people wanting him to solve their problems for them,

who never had to struggle to make time for himself and his Father,

who never felt like he was surrounded by hopeless cases,

who never wanted to unplug his cosmic phone, turn off his pager and make the world go away for just one day, who never wanted to fill up that wine glass just one more time, slouch in his easy chair and smile as the sad faces and whining voices became a blur,

who never wished he'd never taken on the poor, the needy, the wrecks, the shattered, the weak,

who never wondered where he was going to get the strength and patience for the next day, or hour,

who never got livid angry at the leadership of the church for their inane priorities,

who never got tired of listening to people's excuses,

who never wanted to run away from his calling,

who never felt overwhelmed by the endless array of human suffering and sorrow that paraded before him and chased after him,

who never wanted to curl up in the arms of one of his adoring women and be comforted, sheltered from it all for just one night,

who never wanted to be able to close his eyes and pretend he just didn't see that person holding the sign "Will work for food,"

who never wanted to "clean house" and start over with new disciples, and a new low-key, small-scale op-

ONE NIGHT ON THE PHONE

eration,

who never wanted to tell someone, "Use your brain, that's what God gave it to you for!"

who never wanted or needed to bury his head in the pillow and just cry.

Yes, that Jesus.

Maybe that is why my phone is ringing again.

"Steve, this is George. I'm home now. I know I screwed up again. I'm sorry, I really am. Do I still have my job?"

O.K., Jesus. I see.

One more time. Show me how you do this.

CHAPTER TWENTY-SEVEN
BROKEN LEGS

But for you who reverence My name the Sun of Righteousness will rise with healing in its wings; and you will go forth and skip about like calves from the stall.

Malachi 4:2

Today I saw

a woman who looked hard and calloused and very alone eating lunch by herself,

a man running down his co-workers in front of twenty people,

a woman snap at a cashier for not being fast enough,

a man and a woman sitting together speaking in hissing angry whispers,

an elderly couple get on an elevator, she with eyes swollen with tears, he staring silently at the ceiling.

a supervisor cursing at a minimum wage worker,

an executive arrogantly describing how he beat someone into the ground at the last board meeting,

an attractive woman in a very expensive car sitting at a light, staring out her window in tears,

an old man who looked too feeble to walk standing on a corner in 114 degree summer heat holding a sign "will work for food,"

a man boast about a barroom sexual conquest the night before,

a woman with a very blank and hopeless stare pushing a wheelchair with a very old looking young child in it,

a man speeding down the freeway, weaving through the traffic, flipping "the finger" to those who got in his way,

a parent yanking a child around by his arm, cursing at him and calling him stupid,

two women talking about a mutual acquaintance, per-

BROKEN LEGS

haps friend, whom neither could stand,

a man curse his ex-wife,

a wife curse her current husband,

a man in a wheelchair, slumped over, his head half shaved and a long scar from the base of his neck to the top of his head,

a small group of people standing around a time-clock silently waiting for the hour to click, no one smiling,

an angry looking man walking very stiff legged and deliberately down a long corridor, people parting like the Red Sea as he approached,

a woman eating lunch alone, her head bobbing up and down, obviously looking around for someone to sit down with her, but no one ever did,

an elderly lady wandering the hallway lost and too embarrassed to ask for help,

a man with his head down on his arm, who would straighten up once in a while and look to the ceiling as if for help, then lay his head back down,

a very good looking man in the restroom who was combing his hair when I went in and was still combing his hair when I left, a woman on the phone saying over and over in a very low and sad voice, "I know, I understand, I know . . ."

These were all people moving in and out of relationships, some dying, some killing, some fighting to live, some hoping for resurrection.

This is life, the music and the dance. The music of love draws us into the dance, and we move now close, now apart. We touch at the finger-tips, then look away. We move in harmony, we stumble over one another. We embrace, then part. We anticipate the next step, we pull in opposite directions.

The dance is often a sad thing to behold, the symphony is so beautifully written and played, yet the dancers move so erratically and clumsily along. I see the dancers, I watch their halting steps, I see them stagger and fall. I see them trip and crash headlong into one another. I see them lose their partners and wander about searching while others wheel joyously around them. I observed the dance for years not understanding what I was seeing, then one day I fell. From the floor, I was able to see what I could not see before, and in my own pain I finally understood. All the dancers are dancing with broken legs.

Look around you for one day. Watch people. See their faces, look at their bodies, how they move, look at their eyes, watch for the tears just behind their angry brows, their smiles and blank stares. Watch them and know they are wounded dancers. They are broken by sin, their own sins, the sins committed against them, the sins committed against those they love. They know somewhere there is a joyful dance, a glad embrace that moves in harmony with the music but theirs is often a broken dance of fear, guilt, unworthiness, and inadequacy.

It sounds simplistic to say the gospel is the only healing power for the world of broken dancers, yet it is only in the gospel that we know forgiveness, hope, unconditional love, acceptance, healing and joy. It is only when we have been healed of our brokenness by the gospel that we can dance bravely and forgive as we have been forgiven, love as we have been loved, and see the world as God sees it.

When you look at people, do you see, truly see them? We cannot see that they are lost because we ourselves have not been found. We cannot see their broken bones and the hopelessness in their eyes because we have never been healed. We do not understand the power of the gospel because the gospel has never overpowered us. David, murderer, adulterer, overcome by sin, cried out to God in sorrow, "Do not cast me away from your presence and do not take your Holy Spirit from me" (Psalm 51:11). He came to know the power of the gospel, as one so utterly lost in sin who was found by the love of God. But listen, David continues,

> Restore to me the joy of Thy salvation,
> And sustain me with a willing spirit.

> Then I will teach transgressors Thy ways
> And sinners will be converted to Thee.
> Psalm 51:12-12

Only and finally in our hopelessness we can come to know the joy of God's salvation, to be sustained by him in our weakness and brokenness, to be overpowered by the gospel of grace. And we are compelled to see, we cannot help but speak.

David danced with all his might before the Lord when he entered Jerusalem as king. Soon afterwards he crumbled helplessly before the Lord, his bones broken by the guilt of his sin with Bathsheba. He crawled the floor on his face pleading for grace. His was the cry of a broken dancer who knew his only hope for healing was the merciful touch of his God:

> Make me to hear joy and gladness,
> Let the bones which Thou hast broken rejoice.
> Hide Thy face from my sins,
> And blot out all my iniquities.
> Create in me a clean heart, O God,
> And renew a steadfast spirit within me.
> Psalm 51:8-10

It was through grace that David was lifted up and, for the rest of his life, he danced the joyful halting dance of one so in tune with the music and so scarred by his brokenness.

The gospel says we can again hear the joyful sound of the music. There is healing for our broken limbs. We can dance with gladness with one another and before the Lord once more.

CHAPTER TWENTY-EIGHT
CHILDREN . . .

Beloved, let us love one another, for love is from God. . . .

I John 4:7

I spent the night with fifty teenagers last night. It was an all night New Year's Eve party at the church. I was the speaker for the two devotions of the evening.

I went early, even though my first talk was at eleven thirty; I went to watch the kids, truly watch, not just supervise watch. And as I watched I started getting butterflies, scared. I watched:

a bright, giddy, clear-skinned girl who grabbed every opportunity to get in front of the group to clown around, and then at the talent show sang a heartbreaking song about longing for love,

a group of five overweight girls who rarely made a move without each other,

a group of three thin girls who laughed and whispered every time they saw one of the overweight girls participate in an activity,

a sullen pimple-faced boy dressed in the current Bohemian black uniform who sat five feet from people all night,

a very cute girl in tight jeans who sat close to every cute boy she could all night,

a wiry short boy who talked incessantly during activities and escalated his noise even when his friends yelled at him to shut up,

a tall, elegant girl who looked pained as she tried to maintain an air of dignity during the inevitable undignified activities that youth workers think kids will enjoy,

a very, very plain looking girl who tearfully shared the truth within her heart when other kids were spouting off superficial and wise-crack stuff to look cool or get out of sharing with the group,

CHILDREN...

a muscular, clean cut boy who was a Jekyll and Hyde of participation and disruption,

an outgoing, funny girl who, when asked to share her vision for herself for the nineties, became very somber and, while everyone was talking and cutting up, looked at the floor while she talked about loneliness, her family breaking up, her wish to have a car so she could be far away from everything and everybody in her life right now,

a girl who sat in the corner of a pew, eyes red from crying, angrily rejecting people who came by to talk to her.

I watched these and the rest, each with an idiosyncratic mark of adolescence. I thought about what I had planned to say to them about God and I got scared.

I got scared because twenty-three years ago I was an adolescent plague of disruptive outbursts on my own youth ministers and teachers. I knew how merciless kids can be on a speaker they sense is handing them a line of adult sermonic platitudes. I knew how quickly a speaker can lose control of a group of kids, wired by fruit punch, chips and brownies, who think the speaker is phony, out of it, or moralizing to them. It only takes two or three minutes, judgment is passed and you are in or out.

I was scared because most kids don't have the polite self-control adults have. They won't sit in a class and stare blankly at you or the ceiling for thirty minutes and then come, shake you hand, and lie to you saying, "Good lesson." If you watch them during the class you will know immediately if you are accepted or rejected.

But more than all that I got scared because while I watched them I realized, after twenty-two years or so, I really don't have much on them. Sure, I know more "Bible stuff" than they do, but I am still struggling with the same things they were struggling with before my eyes that night; and, to be honest, I'm not sure I'm doing much better than they were.

I watched them and I realized that I still don't know how to love, or even what it really means to be in love. (Every time I think I do something happens and love becomes even more mysterious than before.) I don't know how to reveal myself to people, to drop the phoniness and veneers and ask for help and loving and hugs when I need them. I don't know how to talk intimately with people I love. I don't know how to be loved, accept forgiveness, help and caring. I don't know how to love the unlovely, break out of my comfort zones and circles of like-minded friends. I don't know how to not bow to the idols of my generation. I don't often accept unwanted but good advice from people who are truly more wise than I. I don't know how not to be scared of being hurt. I don't know how to keep from hurting others, either from stupidity or on purpose. I've done too many things I said I'd never do to pretend I can predict my future. I don't understand why God does what he does, or how he does whatever it is he is doing in my life. I am even more in the dark when it comes to God's doing in the lives of those around me.

And as I watched their desperate honesty and self-conscious adolescent seductions I fell in love with them. I abandoned the idea of teaching them and I decided I would love them instead. I found then that I could only pour my heart out to them; I told them what they had taught me. And this is what I learned last night from those fifty kids, goofy with the need for love.

Little children, (and you big children), this is the whole of life: to love God with all your heart, soul, mind and strength, and to love one another. In the end the risks of love, of family, friends or lovers, and even of God, are the same at sixteen as they are at forty: to be honest, to be brave, to be real, to be vulnerable. It is a terrifying risk to love people because you will always be hurt by people you love, you will always hurt people you love. Children, you will long for love, you will give love and be rejected, you will be given love and not know how to accept it.

And if you risk faith, loving God, there will be times you will love God and think he has left you. There will be times you will try to run from God and he will pursue you relentlessly in his holy jealousy.

Little children, stay in awe of this mystery: God is

love. Take the risk, love. It is only when you risk loving as passionately as God loves that his joy is made complete within you. I wish I could tell you it gets easier to love, but it does not. In fact it sometimes gets harder because of the fearful baggage human beings collect through their years. This is true: at forty you will be just as desperate for love as you are at fifteen. At fifty you will be just as afraid of being hurt as you are at sixteen. At sixty God will be as mysterious and unpredictable as he seems at seventeen. And loving God, faith in him, will still only come one way, by the terrifying work of his Spirit within you.

When all of life is said and done, it is about love. And when you feel you are dying for love, dying of love, remember that the mystery of the gospel of Jesus Christ is simply this: God raises the dead because he loves you.